After the Cold War

Russian-American Defense Conversion
for Economic Renewal

Edited by Michael P. Claudon
and Kathryn Wittneben

NEW YORK UNIVERSITY PRESS
New York and London

Library of Congress Cataloging-in-Publication Data

After the Cold War: Russian-American defense conversion for economic
renewal /edited by Michael P. Claudon and Kathryn Wittneben
    p. cm.   (Geonomics Institute for International Economic Advance-
ment series)

    Papers presented at a Geonomics seminar, October 15-18, 1992
    ISBN 0-8147-1488-9 (cloth) — ISBN 0-8147-1489-7 (pbk.)
    1. Economic conversion — Russia — Congresses.
    2. Economic conversion — United States — Congresses.
    I. Claudon, Michael P.   II. Wittneben, Kathryn   III. Series
    HC337.R853D423 1993
    338.4 '0947 — dc20

                                                        92-36328
                                                             CIP

Contents

Acknowledgments

The Geonomics Fall 1992 Gateway Seminar, October 15-18, "Defense Conversion: Achieving U.S.-Russian Cooperation for an Orderly Builddown and Economic Renewal," and the two days of discussion that preceded the seminar were supported by: the American Committee on US-CIS Relations; Booz, Allen & Hamilton; Broadcast Engineering Service; Enterprise Development Information Center, Inc.; Jones International, Inc.; PaineWebber, Inc.; Russian Interpreting Services, Inc.; San Francisco World Trade Associates, Inc.; Scott-European Corporation; and Sheffield Group, Ltd.

Geonomics is also grateful for program support from the Institute's corporate sponsors: Earhart Foundation; Enterprise Development Information Center, Inc.; Heytesbury, Inc.; Willard T. Jackson; Jones International, Inc.; Monsanto Company; Josephine Bay Paul & C. Michael Paul Foundation, Inc.; Scott-European Corporation; and Sharpoint.

And from Institute patrons: Bread Loaf Construction Company, Inc.; Cargill, Inc.; Dun & Bradstreet Corporation Foundation: Ebony Bull Capital Corporation; GTE Spacenet Corporation; Holstein Association; ICI, Inc.; David Klock; Land O'Lakes, Inc.; The Mariska Group, Inc.; Moody's Investors Service; Scott and Aida Pardee; Pfizer International, Inc.; San Francisco World Trade Associations, Inc.; Schooner Capital Corporation; Joseph E. Seagram & Sons, Inc.; Sheffield Group, Ltd.; SOVCAP Ltd.; Summit Limited; and White & Case.

This publication was made possible through support provided by the Office of Private Sector Initiatives, New Independent States Task Force, U.S. Agency for International Development, under Grant No. CCN-0005-G-00-3020-00.

Reducing and converting the military-industrial complexes of the former Soviet Union and the United States will require exceptional resolve, patience, and business acumen in the coming years. Conceptualizing themes, organizing the seminar, and bringing together 60 busy people from points halfway around the world to help speed this process was our immediate test.

We would like to single out three participants for their advice, energy, and enthusiasm: John P. Hardt, associate director of the U.S. Congressional Research Service, for the wealth of his understanding of U.S.-Soviet relations; Kathryn Wittneben for her help in bringing U.S. and Russian military-industrial complex leaders to the discussion; and Aleksei Ponomarev, coordinator of the Interdepartmental Analytical Center in Moscow, who was instrumental in helping us assemble the Russian ministry representatives.

My special thanks to the Geonomics staff and to Nancy Ward, Institute vice president and seminar coordinator, and Robert Waltemyer, the Institute's contract services coordinator, who once again proved that the impossible merely takes a little longer.

As in the past, we deeply appreciate the support of staff, faculty, and students of Middlebury College and the use of the College's Bread Loaf Mountain Campus.

Michael P. Claudon
President
Geonomics Institute

Introduction

The Bread Loaf Charter:
An Action Plan For American-Russian
Partnership in Defense Conversion

Michael P. Claudon

From October 15-18, 1992, 60 Russians, Americans, and Canadians came together for Geonomics' Fall Seminar to discuss the obstacles and opportunities in reversing decades of military buildup and in converting defense industries to civilian production. During the three days, the participants — senior officials from Russia's five key ministries involved in defense conversion; senior members representing the U.S. Departments of State, Commerce, and Defense, and the Agency for International Development; American and Russian defense conversion experts and business people — found that they shared a common concern: defense conversion, despite its critical importance to the political and economic security of both countries, is moving far too slowly.

Military build-down and economic renewal based on the transfer of defense industry assets to private hands is possible, but only if both sides work cooperatively and aggressively to create the political, economic, and military framework for conversion. Toward that end, seminar participants agreed in the Bread Loaf Charter on a set of guiding principles and recommended that two task forces develop proposals to deal with specific military, economic, and political concerns.

A Follow-up to June Summit

The specific recommendations of the Bread Loaf Charter build on the general goals of the Charter for American-Russian Partnership and Friendship signed at the Bush-Yeltsin Summit last June and on supporting defense conversion legislation. While the Partnership Charter has spawned new programs, such as the Department of Commerce's new BISNIS program that encourages investment in Russia, seminar participants agreed that cooperative efforts must be expanded.

Timely Action Is Critical

The NIS and the West can ill afford a protracted debate on appropriate courses of action. Mounting misery and poverty are testing the limits of Russian peoples' patience with economic reforms.

Despite this growing political and economic crisis, Western pledges of support have not always been followed by technical assistance programs or the extension of loans and credits. Twenty-two countries and multilateral institutions are now operating at least 230 different aid programs in Russia, but IMF and World Bank officials admit that commitments are increasingly lagging behind promises. The G-7 countries and IMF have pledged $24 billion in aid, credits, and deferment of foreign debt payments, but red tape, concerns over the progress of economic reform and foreign debt payments have delayed or stopped many programs.

Conversion in both countries will ultimately cost billions of dollars, billions that neither the Russian nor American governments nor multilateral institutions have. The Charter for Russian-American Friendship and Partnership and the Bread Loaf Charter do not attempt to fund conversion through government aid. Rather, the charters attempt to help create the legal, political, and social infrastructure needed to encourage private and enterprise investment. Russian ministry officials stressed at the seminar that they understood our budgetary constraints and argued that low-cost technical assistance would be most helpful for both sides.

The Russian government must provide technical support and some transitional funding, but conversion will ultimately take place at the regional and enterprise level and must be financed from enterprise profits. The enterprises themselves are learning to live without state orders and are trying to develop products that meet consumer needs.

Appropriations under the Freedom Support Act are on the right track. Up to $400 million will be available to the U.S. Department of Defense for purposes authorized under the Former Soviet Union Demilitarization Act of 1992. Of that total, $40 million will be available for conversion of NIS defense industries; $15 million is allocated to military-to-military contacts and personnel requalification; $25 million will be available for joint research programs. Up to $50 million can be spent on the Multilateral Nuclear Safety Initiative. These appropriations are a significant first step and are psychologically and politically important.

Monetary Policy Is Not Enough

In a significant break with the policies of the G-7 countries and the IMF, the framers of the Bread Loaf Charter called for a partnership that goes well beyond narrowly focused monetary stabilization programs. Defense conversion and economic reform must include specific attention to individual and mutual national security concerns and international affairs, in addition to economics. Monetarist economists notwithstanding, monetary stabilization is necessary but not sufficient to deal with Russia's economic and political problems.

A central theme of the Bread Loaf Charter is that we face interconnected political, security, and economic problems that require prompt, joint action. Articulating new mutually agreeable military doctrines that reflect the new post-Cold War security environment, for example, is an essential precondition for a partnership in defense conversion. Similarly, privatization of defense enterprises is an essential precondition to attract foreign investment in defense conversion.

Business Task Force Is Needed

The group, and especially the Russian and American businessmen involved in commercial spinoffs from former defense plants, argued energetically that joint defense conversion projects present long-term opportunities for U.S. business. Toward that end the Bread Loaf Charter calls for a U.S.-Russian business working group to develop strategies to generate mutually beneficial trade and investment that promotes defense conversion.

That economic renewal and military conversion are strongly complementary, not conflicting, activities, was a theme we heard repeatedly from all constituencies at the seminar.

Russian defense enterprises represent Russia's best technology, most highly trained work force, and most modern production facilities. In Russia, where the military sector once employed one out of every five workers, accounts for 20 percent of the GNP, and 80 percent of all R & D personnel, defense conversion is the key to successful economic reform. Since the best assets are in Russia's defense sector, the greatest potential for short-term progress lies in converting and privatizing the defense sector.

As the deputy general director of Russia's leading "Star Wars" firm put it, "During years of defense research and development we have come up with many distinguished discoveries, but they are raw diamonds. You have great technological threats from Japan; this is the best time to cut them together."

Government officials and business people alike believe that joint commercial projects could very well represent the future trend of increased cooperation between our two countries. The American investor benefits from Russia's technology, such as in advanced computer software, and trained workforce and gains access to the country's huge domestic market. The Russian enterprise learns Western marketing skills and production techniques needed to compete in international markets.

But there are many unresolved questions in possible high-technology partnerships and in global competition for high-technology markets. Where does the United States want to cooperate with Russia and where does it want to compete, ministry officials asked. Will the United States, for example, accept competition in areas which it has monopolized, such as space services?

Improve Infrastructure

While there is growing interest in business opportunities in Russia, the lack of an appropriate legal and institutional framework continues to discourage investors. In the last half year, the Russian government has adopted nearly two dozen laws, protecting patents and trademarks, computer programs, and data bases. These should help normalize technology transfers. But the work is far from complete, especially in defining and valuing intellectual property. The Bread Loaf Charter calls for much more rapid progress creating a Western-style legal and business infrastructure.

Russia also badly lacks modern telephone and computer communications. It needs to establish institutional mechanisms to support commercial payments; insurance and land title guarantees; dissemination and application of business legislation; and appraisal and valuation of buildings, land, stock, bonds. In short, Russia needs continuing help in creating the necessary infrastructure for commercial operations. Consistent, not arbitrary, application of legislation and regulations is essential to a partnership for defense conversion.

Shrink the Defense Complex

A smaller, more stable, and well-defined defense complex in Russia is clearly in the national interest of the United States. The prospect of uncontrolled exports of defense equipment and technology and the emigration of nuclear specialists to the Third World is a frightening sequel to the end of the Cold War.

Herein lies the catch-22. There is very little political will to downsize the U.S. military sector rapidly until Russia makes significantly greater progress with its own demilitarization program. But, Russian success depends directly on Western technical assistance, access to current technologies, and lowered trade barriers, and Western aid has been slowed by the global recession, domestic priorities, red tape, and the lack of concrete programs in Russia.

Both sides must be sensitive to the need to balance national and international security requirements with their economic interests. It is critical, as the Bread Loaf Charter argues, that military authorities and security officials discuss and understand each other's security needs, agree upon the level of their armed forces, and develop strict regulations on the export of arms. Without such discussion and agreement on military doctrines, it will be difficult for both sides to build support to move aggressively in reducing the size of their armed forces and military-industrial complex.

Joint discussions are particularly important given the pressure on the Russian government and defense enterprises to sell arms to the Third World to raise critical hard currency and to keep the military industrial complex afloat. Arms sales, such as the sale of Russian submarines to Iran, Mig-29s to Malaysia, or helicopters to Turkey are potentially destabilizing and highlight the need to avoid cut-rate competition and the creation of an international arms bazaar.

Rethink COCOM

Converting defense industries and retraining enterprise and military personnel for new jobs in civilian industries offer great promise for U.S.-Russian cooperation. There are numerous opportunities for the U.S. in training, technology transfer, and retooling and redirecting defense industries into producing vital consumer and agro-industrial sector goods.

In this regard, Russian business people and policymakers argued passionately that greater access to current Western technology is critical to the modernization of their infrastructure. The Commerce Department has eliminated export restrictions on about three-quarters of its dual-technology list in the past two years and now operates on a "presumption of approval" rather than a "presumption of denial" in evaluating export requests.

But the Russian participants expressed severe irritation by what they consider to be lingering Cold War attitudes that continue to restrict export of dual-use technologies in such areas as fiber optics, telecommunications, and high-speed computers. Many Russian policymakers believe that they are being permitted access only to outdated technology, particularly in telecommunications and transportation. This lack of trust and access to technology is a "national put down," one ministry official complained.

Such advanced technology is critical if Russia is to compete in international markets and to attract Western investment. Toward that end, the Bread Loaf Charter places a high priority on developing mechanisms to promote productivity, competitiveness, and technology exchange.

Establishing the COCOM (Coordinating Committee on Multilateral Export Controls) Cooperation Forum at the June Summit is an important step. The forum, which is scheduled to hold its first meeting in November, provides the West and the NIS with the bilateral framework for discussing export controls and to coordinate technical assistance efforts. It is critical that the Forum move aggressively to review restrictions, to remove restrictions where possible, and to place safeguards on the use of dual-use technology. It is equally important that the Departments of Commerce and State, which are not bound by the "gentlemen's agreements" of COCOM, also review remaining export controls on dual-use and military technologies.

Russia's inability to service its $80 billion foreign debt highlights the need for the country to broaden its export base and to capitalize on its high-technology resources. If Russia is to be an international economic power, it must emphasize the export of high-tech manufactured goods and services and reduce the uncontrolled export of strategic raw materials.

Cooperation Is in Our Interest

Good intentions and calls for cooperation are not enough. It is time to convert good intentions into solid programs for defense conversion and mutual economic renewal.

• In assisting in the reduction of their military capabilities, we, too, can transfer resources from our military to productive civilian uses;

• In helping dismantle a confrontational, military-based foreign policy, we benefit from a cooperative, law-based international system;

• In aiding their economic and political transformation, we create profitable trade and investment abroad and economic growth at home.

The gravest threat is that we fail to take advantage of this historic opportunity.   ↳

Seminar Papers

The specific recommendations contained in the Bread Loaf Charter, which follows, were distilled from three days' of energetic deliberation and debate. The papers and reports in this volume were catalysts for this debate and provided fresh information and insights into the defense conversion challenge.

The volume begins by looking at defense conversion from the perspective of the government policymaker and ends with the ground-level views of Russian enterprise managers and American businesspeople.

Section I provides an overview of defense conversion, with particular attention paid to assessing the prospects for U.S.-Russian cooperation in defense conversion, economic reform, and defense conversion strategies.

Section II offers a series of high-level views of defense conversion presented by the five ministries specifically involved in Russian defense conversion: defense, economics and finance, foreign affairs, foreign economic relations, and science.

Section III narrows the focus and examines Russian defense conversion from the perspective of individual Russian defense enterprises and organizations involved in preparing decommissioned military officers for work in the civilian sector.

Section IV contains a critical examination of the role U.S. business can play in Russian defense conversion and a frank analysis from an American businessperson of opportunities in defense conversion in Russia.

The Charter*

On October 14-18, 1992, the undersigned group of private citizens of Russia, United States, and Canada, agreed during the Geonomics Institute's Fall Gateway Seminar to a set of principles and recommended actions for the leaders of Russia and the United States. These recommendations build on the Charter for Russian-American Partnership and Friendship and related supporting legislation in both countries.

It is critical that we find mutually acceptable ways of removing barriers to technology transfer and joint development of technology processes, within the context of a mutual safeguard and proliferation control regime appropriate to the new security environment. In view of the critical need for course corrections in each country's current policy to conform with the principles of these statements and proceed forthwith to implement necessary action programs, a series of specific understandings were reached.

Critical global political, security, and economic conditions require joint action in conversion and economic restructuring. A set of problems must be addressed to put these major countries on a new, more positive course.

• To develop a detailed program in order to reemploy released military manpower, defense industry employees, and physical assets for production of civilian goods and services.

• To reach understanding of the concepts and doctrines underpinning respective national security.

• To identify programs at the company and enterprise levels and varying territorial jurisdictions that are mutually beneficial in promoting employment and profit.

• To effectuate effective conversion, and rapid and extensive privatization in Russia, it is necessary to redirect and restructure domestic assets and to attract foreign investment. Particular attention must be given to the redirection and retraining of the military related human assets to new productive civilian tasks.

• To release major constraints on financing through prompt and definitive relief of the debt burden on the Russian economy; the facilitation of funding by national, multinational, and other organizations of targeted programs; and the creation of a favorable private investment climate.

• To change restrictive legislation and the regulatory climate in both countries consistent with the needs of the new cooperative environment.

To bring about these actions of the Charter specific steps should be undertaken:

• Convene a group of responsible authorities and experts of both nations to define agreeable principles of mutual security, to agree upon specific actions to implement those principles, and to ensure that such actions further our stated objectives of defense conversion and economic renewal.

• Task a United States-Russian business working group with developing detailed strategies to generate maximum mutually beneficial trade and investment between the two countries facilitated by the defense conversion process. Included in this task is the goal of developing and enhancing transparent legal and regulatory structures in both countries.

The participants plan to continue their dialogue and call upon their respective governments, businesses, and research organizations to take prompt action on these matters of critical importance. ↳

---

* A list of seminar participants who signed the Charter is available from Geonomics.

Defense Conversion: An Overview

Kathryn Wittneben

Defense conversion may well be the lever that makes or breaks economic reforms in Russia. This is so because of the impact of the defense industry on Russia's economy, where 25 percent of Russia's work force is employed.

Since the breakup of the former Soviet Union (FSU), the military-industrial complex has experienced major upheavals. The dissolution of the country caused the abrupt cancellation of massive state military orders. This led to the technical bankruptcy of a majority of former defense enterprises, the closing of factories, and the laying off of hundreds of thousands of workers, with a projected unemployment of five to seven million workers in 1993. With no (or little) state funding available to subsidize continuing production or employees' salaries, most defense-related enterprises have had to try to convert from military to civilian production almost overnight.

This predicament has created pressure on the Russian government to continue subsidizing defense enterprises and to allow them to expand arms exports. The Russian government is developing its policies and programs to support defense conversion, while it is struggling to carry out its massive economic reforms and privatization process.

Russian Conversion Policy

The Russian government's policy on conversion is presently undergoing review and possible revision. The current basis for conversion is the Law on the Conversion of the Defense Industry, adopted by the Russian Supreme Soviet in March 1992, that defines conversion in Article 1 as "partial or full reorientation of freed production capacities, scientific and technical potential, and labor resources of defense and related enterprises from military to civil needs."

Within the boundaries of this law, the goals of Russian conversion are to: 1) Preserve the most important elements of production and scientific-technical potential from the Russian defense complex; 2) Reorient these elements for the modernization and reconstruction of the economy and its social sphere, emphasizing import substitution and the expansion of exports.

The main role in carrying out this conversion is assigned to defense enterprises as a voluntary activity that is encouraged by tax and other concessions. The government declares its intention to establish a state conversion fund. Participation by foreign investors in the conversion and privatization of defense enterprises is made possible under specific terms and conditions within the State Privatization Program, the Russian Law "On Foreign Investments in the RSFSR," and Russian legislation on privatization. Social services are continued for workers with at least 15 years in the defense sector. Going further, cities where more than 20% of the population becomes unemployed as a result of conversion may be declared priority development territories. Provision is also made for regional organs to draw up their own conversion programs. Finally, export controls are to be imposed on the transfer of technologies that could be used in the creation of weapons of mass destruction. (See Appendices 2 and 3 for the full text of the Russian conversion law and the corresponding resolution of the Supreme Soviet.).

Many of the foregoing provisions are elaborated in a new draft legislative chapter on defense conversion that was presented to the Russian Federation Supreme Soviet during the fall of 1992 for consideration. A number of hearings on defense conversion were held by the Supreme Soviet during the fall of 1992.

The Russian Government Strategy on Conversion

The new draft chapter on conversion, as well as other papers on the subject that have been prepared by the Russian Interdepartmental Analytical Center and other officials, spell out a proposed government strategy. There appears to be some agreement within the government that conversion must take place within the context of economic reform and that it must occur step by step. The role of private enterprise is viewed in this perspective as critical to the process, with the main role of government being to provide the framework within which conversion takes place.

These views are not, however, accepted by everyone within the govern-

ment, and particularly not in the Supreme Soviet. Despite the fact that it is
the legislation on defense conversion that provides its foundation, there is
still little agreement between the government and the Supreme Soviet on
the aims of conversion and how to carry it out.

The official government strategy is made up of five measures:

1. Continued state support in priority areas and for priority projects.
Government support is called on to help preserve the scientific-technologi-
cal potential of the Russian defense complex; support import-substituting
and export-oriented industries; and assist ongoing defense enterprises to
maximize their use of "dual use" technologies and become more market-
oriented.

The government, through various ministries, has been developing lists
of favored industries. The latest version of this list, found in the draft chapter
on defense conversion, includes equipment and technologies in the following sectors: food processing, construction, pharmaceuticals and medicine,
energy and the environment, timber production, civil aviation, shipbuilding, microelectronics and special materials. Emphasis is placed on high-
technology industries because it is believed that they may be best able to
generate hard currencies. The government also proposes to target research
and development, with an emphasis on market-oriented results including
export promotion activities.

What is important to note is that consumer-oriented industries are not
included in this draft priority list. This is because the government has scarce
financial resources, and can only support so much. The aim is that consumer needs should be met through the establishment of a market economy
and private enterprise.

2. Reduced support for obsolete industries. There is vigorous debate
among the ministries (particularly between the Ministry of Defense and the
former Ministry of Industry) regarding what industries and/or enterprises
should be "allowed to die." This debate is closely related to the development
of Russia's first defense mobilization strategy and defense budget. (The
debate is similar to the one that has taken place in the U.S. Congress over
the past decade on whether there are strategic industries which should be
maintained through government support).

**3. Development of the necessary infrastructure to support conversion,
including the economic, legal and regulatory framework.** This includes the
establishment of a sound export control regime that meets the requirements of COCOM (Coordinating Committee for Multilateral Export Controls), in which Russia has requested membership.

4. Elimination of barriers to conversion. The Russian Interdepartmental Analytical Center, in conjunction with the various ministerial conversion

departments, is developing a list of such barriers—both internal and external—to be addressed by the government.

5. Provision of tax and other concessions to enterprises undergoing conversion. The law on defense conversion sets out specific concessions. In addition, the Ministry of Foreign Economic Relations has indicated a strong interest in supporting the development of small business, particularly small high-tech firms, through tax preferences and other assistance.

Pavel Yelkin, director of the Division For High-Tech Export and Defense Conversion, Ministry of Foreign Economic Relations, gives an example of the former closed city of Tomsk #7, which produced plutonium for nuclear plants. The city has a population of 100,000, with no alternative employment available outside of the defense industry. The city requested 500 to 600 million rubles from the Russian government to assist in carrying out conversion. Since funds of that order were not available, the employees instead asked for and got equipment and other assistance to help start small businesses. Yelkin and others now propose that similar assistance should be provided to other municipalities that are willing to show a comparable initiative.

It is unclear as yet whether the government's draft chapter on defense conversion will be adopted by the Supreme Soviet. The speaker of the Russian Parliament, Ruslan I. Khasbulatov, has advocated a more gradual approach to economic reform, with more assistance to defense enterprises over a longer period of time. Mikhail Bazhanov, who used to head the State Committee on Conversion, criticized the government's conversion policy in July 1992 and stated that the rate of conversion need not exceed 3 percent per year, as compared to the 70 percent being pursued in the past two years.

Russian Administrative Structure to Support Conversion

The Russian government has been undergoing substantial changes during 1992 with respect to who is in charge of developing and implementing its policies and programs on conversion. At the present time, there are seven Russian ministries, in addition to other government-related groups, that have some authority and responsibility for particular aspects of conversion. Consequently, the decision-making process is quite fluid.

The attached diagram presents the structure of the Russian Administration with respect to conversion as of December 1992. Since it is often difficult for U.S. business people to understand the Russian government's involvement in conversion, the current major roles for each of the departments are given below.

Executive Branch of the Russian Government: Defense Conversion

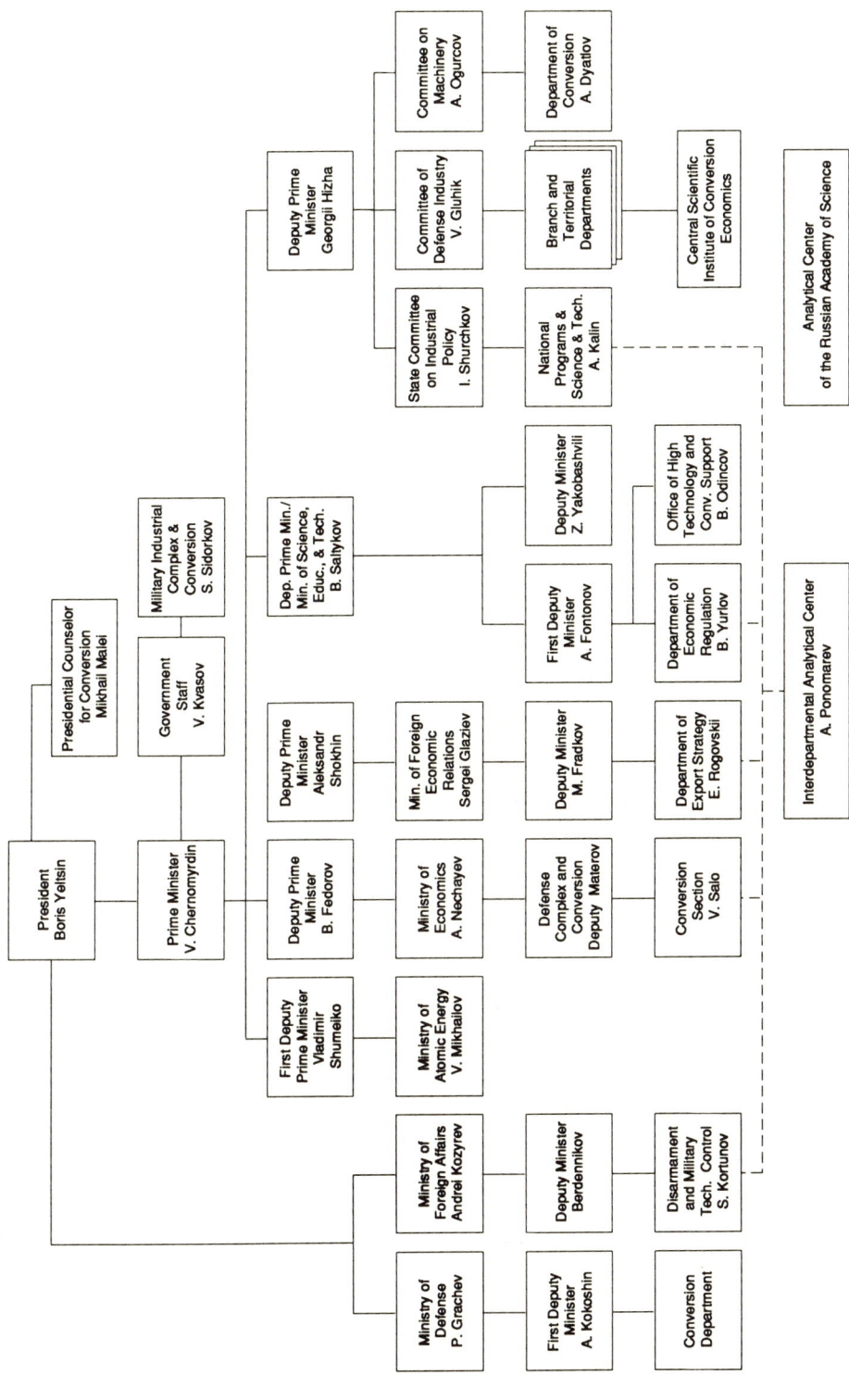

Ministry of Foreign Economic Relations. The ministry has a special strategic unit that is identifying enterprises and technologies in the defense sector that might become prime candidates for the preparation of technical proposals. Such proposals could form the basis of business plans for joint ventures with foreign firms.

The Ministry's Department of Export Strategy is involved in developing export promotion activities and is also looking at ways to develop large-scale international projects, using Russian technology and defense enterprises, that could be funded by a group of countries or an international organization. These projects would include an emphasis on conversion.

Ministry of Foreign Affairs. The ministry is responsible for representing Russia's foreign interests and conducting international negotiations on issues connected to conversion, such as arms limitation. It is nominally the lead agency for the Safe Secure Dismantlement talks with the U.S. government, although the Ministry of Atomic Energy takes the technical lead in these talks.

Ministry of Science, Higher Education, and Technical Policy. The ministry is involved in deciding which large-scale scientific initiatives are to be budgeted. It has two offices that focus on conversion-related issues. The Department of Economic Regulation is particularly concerned with the maintenance of Russia's scientific and technological base.

Ministry of Economy. The ministry is developing, together with the Ministry of Defense, the projected military force requirements as a basis for the state defense budget and state military orders. The Department of Defense Complex and Conversion in the Ministry of Economy is responsible for the defense budget and the allocation of government funds for conversion.

State Commission for Industrial Policy. The former Ministry of Industry was dissolved at the end of September 1992. In its place is a new State Commission for Industrial Policy, along with four separate industrial branches. The relationships among the State Commission and the industrial branches are not yet developed; the status and organization of these industrial branches have also not been determined. It is expected that some of the responsibilities of the former Ministry of Industry will be carried out by the State Commission, and that its responsibilities will include assistance in the development of the government's policy and strategies on conversion.

Ministry of Atomic Energy. The ministry continues to oversee the defense enterprises and institutes that work with atomic energy and nuclear weapons production. This ministry is involved in approving large-scale international projects and joint ventures with foreign partners, if the proposed project involves one of the enterprises or institutes within its jurisdiction. Each nuclear department within the ministry has its own conversion specialist.

Ministry of Defense. The ministry is primarily responsible for the development and implementation of Russia's defense policy, along with government procurement of weapons and other military-related production.

State Counselor on Conversion Mikhail Malei. The counselor serves as a personal advisor to President Yeltsin on conversion. He has a very small staff and interacts on an ad hoc basis with the various Ministers on specific defense conversion issues.

Interdepartmental Analytical Center. The center was created to assist four ministries in the development of the government's policies on defense conversion. It is primarily funded by the government, although it is a quasi-governmental group. Its primary responsibilities are to develop a comprehensive data-base on the Russian defense sector; assist in the development of the government's defense conversion policies; and make recommendations to the government and others on how to plan and finance conversion, the types of legal and regulatory structures that are required to assist in carrying out conversion, and the type of information that needs to be developed at the enterprise level to attract foreign investment.

It is difficult to determine just when each of the above ministries and departments becomes involved in a conversion project that includes a foreign partner. When this question was put to the relevant deputy ministers and department heads, the answer was that "it depends on the particular project." In general, if the project is large, involving millions of dollars and a partnership with a large or strategically important defense enterprise, a number of ministries may become involved.

Aleksei Ponomarev, director of the Interdepartmental Analytical Center, advised that a U.S. company should first identify and establish a relationship with the enterprise or plant with which it can work. It is the responsibility of that enterprise to obtain the necessary permissions and support from the ministries and higher levels within the Administration. It appears that deputy prime ministers, and deputy ministers may or may not become involved in supporting a particular project depending on their level of interest, where the project is being carried out (for example, whether it involves a plant in his/her home district), and other political and economic factors. U.S. companies should be prepared, however, to work with their Russian partners to identify and obtain appropriate government support.

Implications for the United States

Defense conversion in Russia and Ukraine has important implications for U.S. national security and foreign policy. The demilitarization and denuclearization of the FSU are two established U.S. goals, to which the conversion of excess defense production capacity is obviously linked. Furthermore, as Russian military strength decreases, the way should be opened for additional cuts in the U.S. defense budget, which would release valuable U.S. resources for nondefense purposes.

Russian defense conversion should also produce economic benefits for the United States by creating new opportunities for U.S. trade and investment. American CEOs and technical experts believe that doing business with Russian and Ukrainian defense enterprises will enhance U.S. competitiveness in certain high-technology and other industries. This issue will be examined more in Part Three.

Part One lays out the major policy issues that are presently facing the Russian government with respect to conversion. Dr. John Hardt's piece focuses on the overall framework for developing and carrying out conversion in Russia, along with the need for greater U.S. government cooperation in this area. He argues that Russian policy should be based on the concept of economic renewal, with emphasis on improving the quality of life, environment, health, and housing. His article provides a blueprint to facilitate the process of change (or conversion) in Russia.

Dr. Aleksei Ponomarev emphasizes the importance of greater Russian-U.S. business cooperation in conversion. He outlines the problems that have hindered such cooperation and identifies the steps being taken by the Russian government and enterprises to overcome these obstacles. The articles by Russian Minister for Foreign Economic Relations Sergei Glaziev and Deputy Minister of Economics and Finance Ivan Materov provide additional insights into the Russian government's policymaking process and issues with respect to conversion.

1

Achieving U.S.-Russian Cooperation for an Orderly Build-down and Economic Renewal

John P. Hardt

W e are in the process of radical revolutionary change where the great adversaries of recent years are now potential military and economic partners. In that sense, defense conversion is at the heart of a successful economic transition and partnership. But we are profoundly uncertain about how to proceed, what to expect, and how to get results.

The Russian and other transforming economies have largely adopted the Western economic model that attempts to provide rising real incomes, employment opportunities, and a stable monetary environment. That's simple to state, but as we can see in Russia and the other newly independent states, difficult to achieve.

With its abundant natural resources and skilled manpower, Russia is putatively the richest country in the world . But this wealth has been used to create a military superpower and to consolidate the power of the Government and the Party. The challenge is to redirect the resources of the defense industrial complex. Willy Sutton used to say, "I like the banks, because that's where the money is." We must look at the defense industrial complex, because that's where their best human resources are.

For generations, they have channeled the best and the brightest and given top priority to the defense complex. The Sakharovs of the past produced bombs and the ingredients to be a military superpower. Simplifying again, Russia must redirect these human assets if it is to effectively restructure its economy. The consumer, Ivan Ivanovich, and his desire to

The author's views are his own, not necessarily those of the U.S. Congress, Congressional Research Service of the Library of Congress, or the U.S. government.

live better must now be given top priority over expanding the state's power.

We have a parallel in the Renaissance where the Medicis hired Leonardo DaVinci to prepare fortifications and battering rams to knock down defenses. Fortunately, he was able later to redirect his resources to being a creative artist.

But Russia is also facing revolutionary changes with no real parallel in history. Never has a country faced the need to rapidly make so many profound changes in governance, bilateral and multilateral relationships. It's almost like Christopher Columbus setting out for the New World. In Russia, one-sixth of the earth's surface, we have a country attempting to develop simultaneously a free market and a pluralistic society based on the rule of law.

The Synergy of Democracy and Free Markets

Linking market and resource development and job creation requires a democratic market. This has been the tradition and lessons of the Western transformation. It is important that Russia follows this synergistic model of democratic, pluralistic development. A market place for goods is fostered by a market place for ideas — "one man, one vote." Russia needs democratic leadership, but it must be strong democratic leadership. This may seem contradictory, but strong leadership is needed to build the broad support and consensus, which is essential for the success of revolutionary transformation.

In business terms, little can be done to attract foreign investment unless there is political stability and a predictable legal environment. Responsible leadership that can be held accountable is needed to guide the process in a predictable fashion. Having spent a good deal of time recently in the Russian Parliament, I can speak to the problem of political diversity and accountability there; strong, accountable, and inclusive leadership is essential to provide the political base for effective economic restructuring and defense conversion. Factions can issue decrees but ultimately cannot implement them without the support of the industrialists, the military, the agricultural interests, the people, and the cities; the separation of power and a political consensus must be built on a broad-based functional consensus for effective policy implementation.

In restructuring a system dominated by the military to a civilian-oriented, open economy, we must look at the political underpinnings of that system. Is there a framework that can be borrowed from other countries? Reactionary parts of the Civic Union, reflecting the interests of many industrialists, are attracted by the Chinese model of a vigorous free market under strong autocratic leadership with arbitrary police power. Some, like President Nazarbayev in Kazakhstan, look to the South Korean model where there is market development and a very strong autocratic government hand, supported by the police. In effect, they support retention of the political control of the old system but move toward the market on the economic side. An undemocratic market transition in Russia is not supportable by domestic or Western forces.

DeGaulle's France: A Model for Development?

A better model is the DeGaulle model. DeGaulle in the Fifth Republic established an inclusive government, a government made up largely of non-Gaullists. DeGaulle's government ended the war and the empire, and reformed, restructured, and reduced the military. He brought the former members of the French empire into some degree of comity and turned the country toward developed Western markets. And he did that with a domestic program, designed by a liberal economist, that was supported by industrialists and a broad cross-section of people in the society. Moreover, he introduced a new tax code, reformed agriculture, and continued the process that he had undertaken in 1944: establishment of an independent, professional civil service.

These historical developments provide useful insight for Russian leaders. The experience of France is not directly translatable, either from the French to the Russian, or from France as a country to Russia. But the point is that we need to think about the Russian transformation in a democratic context. These changes require strong, inclusive, and effective leadership that can implement participatory policies. A strong, inclusive democratic coalition is needed for this transformation, not a dictatorship.

Many opposition reform groups called for a broad renewal program. Comprehensive patriotic renewal means more than support of monetary stabilization. Beyond attacking inflation, the government must address the problems of consumer goods production, productivity, income, and employment.

This program requires not only strong domestic leadership, but also cooperation and technical help from the West and especially the leadership of the United States. The Charter for American-Russian Partnership and Friendship signed at the June 1992 summit provides such a framework for cooperative programs and technical assistance.

In its comprehensive restructuring, Russia must focus on programs that benefit the people in the short term, as well as the long term. These programs must improve the food supply at affordable prices, increase the productivity of the energy sector, improve medical care, clean up the environment, and increase good housing for returning military and the public. If citizens are to give their consent to be governed and are to participate fully in the process, they must have performance from their government. If they do not see immediate tangible performance, they must, at least, believe that the future will be better. Inflation, few goods in the stores, and a prospect of high unemployment with little prospect for improvement do not generate confidence in the government.

Conversion: A New Patriotic Goal for Russia

A new conversion strategy should shift productive scientists and manpower, no longer required for defense programs, to competitive, consumer-related programs that would improve productivity and the quality of life. Establishing the Soviet Union as a military world power was a patriotic effort; transforming the country and building a better society is an equally appropriate, new patriotic goal.

By supporting this comprehensive restructuring, President Yeltsin can rekindle a sense of patriotism and redefine national security in economic and social terms. Without this redirection, Russia cannot become competitive in the global marketplace. Again, the defense establishment is at the heart of restructuring, because that's where the best assets are for competing in consumer goods markets.

The precondition for initiating successful defense conversion is developing better information about the military-industrial complex. The government has purposely concealed the extent of its military activities and assets. A complete inventory of these assets is needed so that the government can decide what must be retained to support the military and what may be converted.

It is critical to move assets into productive civilian activities and equally important do it in a way that minimizes unemployment. If the government does not treat employment as an important human value, it will be required to treat it as an important political value. Government leaders who disregard the impact of mass unemployment are likely to be out of office. No government in Central Europe has been reelected after introducing so-called shock therapy.

Initially, conversion specialists must distinguish between enterprises producing civilian goods and that are not dependent on state defense orders and those enterprises that are needed to meet future defense needs. Three categories of defense industrial enterprises should be supported by the state budget or released for privatization.

1. Enterprises primarily producing civilian or consumer goods under Defense Ministry jurisdiction. These major producers of civilian goods could become competitive with prudent availability of state credit, some restructuring, and expanded non-defense output. The goal would be to privatize these newly competitive enterprises as rapidly as feasible.

2. Research and production enterprises that have a reasonable chance for joint ventures with foreign firms should become privatized enterprises. These enterprises would require some restructuring to become efficient producers for foreign and domestic markets whether or not they become joint ventures. State credit and foreign assistance would be needed in the short run. Some enterprises, such as those in joint space activities, might remain state supported in the longer term or seek foreign partners.

Foreign assistance should be sought and funding could be provided for the first two categories on a phased, conditional basis. The purpose would be to make the enterprises self-financing at as early a date as possible or move toward closing them. State funding to keep category 2 afloat could proceed with aggressive restructuring efforts to create competitive enterprises or to proceed toward privatization.

3. Research and production enterprises needed to produce military items for projected military forces with allowance for mobilization or surge capacity should remain state enterprises on the state budget. The currently projected force levels, a fraction of former levels, should have assured state funding and orders within a future phased-down requirement, e.g., a five-year force development plan. Precise judgments on the retention and state support of enterprises may not initially be necessary. Timely reduction of the massive defense burden on the state budget is more critical. A phased reduction would also provide some certainty of employment for workers, scientists, managers, and communities for meeting continuing defense needs.

The third category should be clearly and definitively established so that state financing for force development can be planned, debated, and approved by the parliament in a multi-year defense budget. More tax revenue may be necessary depending on the political judgment on what force development is required. A value-added tax dedicated to defense conversion/renewal like the U.S. gas tax dedicated to roads might be an innovative revenue source.

This step would then "blue-line" (certify for retention and support) a small portion of the current defense industrial assets. With this process and revenue base, workers, scientists, managers, and communities could all be reassured that funding and employment would be assured for at least a specific time period with credible criteria for extension. This planned capacity could then limit production for Russian military needs, not foreign arms sales.

The majority of defense production capacity would be "red-lined" or eliminated. This is capacity, primarily developed for producing military hardware, that cannot be economically converted to produce civilian goods. While much of the plant and equipment is not convertible, the scientists and workers could be retrained and protected with an effective safety net during the transition to new employment.

The challenge is to identify those elements that can compete in a market and to provide an effective and efficient way to move them to new firms. If these assets can be used productively to meet domestic needs and to earn hard currency, they will attract the interest of private investors and international organizations that support private enterprise, like the European Bank for Reconstruction and Finance and the many activities of the World Bank family.

In some cases, investment might not provide immediate market returns but would improve the quality of life, environment, health, and housing or facilitate the process of change. Although not likely to be funded from the market, these needs are socially important. Few indicators rank higher in public opinion polls than those involving the quality of life. Few potential investors would not rank improving the infrastructure as a key factor in attracting new investment. Projects could be ranked by their potential to resolve urgent ecological and health problems in each community, to generate jobs, or to save money. Beneficial employment-creating projects should be contrasted with safety net payments to enterprises that do not provide employment or produce valuable products or services.

The current retention of staffs, funded by inflationary monetary policy, should not be acceptable either for domestic or international support. Prudent funding and staffing of quality of life and infrastructure projects require international funding, domestic financing, and local support. These activities would not be self financed and broad-based support would be essential.

The link between international and domestic funding could be matching funds; for example, the Udmurtia region could be informed that they could qualify for some international funding for health, environment, or housing projects if they provided some of the funding from Russian state or local taxation. Additional ruble funding might be arranged from innovative repayment or conversion of old Soviet debts and the Lend–Lease Settlement. In any event, the credit creation should be restructured to keep down the real interest rate so as to promote domestic and foreign investment.

At the national level, President Yeltsin might appeal for a national renewal program that draws on the best scientific talent to meet the nation's pressing problems: reverse the decline in health standards, change ecocide to environmental protection, provide adequate housing in place of dwelling space below the European sanitary norm, and become an efficient economy capable of becoming competitive internationally. This job-creating program could be supplemented by volunteer national service and new value-added taxes to be targeted to correct food, energy, and environmental shortages and problems. Moreover, human resources from the defense sector could be redirected along with supplies of goods and equipment: military builders could be shifted to the food and energy sectors; strategic reserves could be used to meet critical civilian needs.

In short, this could be a patriotic mobilization effort to renew not only the quality of the Russian economy, but its spirit and pride. If the transition is not developed in these terms, it will be difficult to gain the support of the people and to justify foreign, multinational, and international involvement and funding. The IMF and the World Bank, for example, may be planning to increase their funding support for restructuring and market-oriented programs to as much as $3 billion a year — about the annual financing level of India and Indonesia — if Russia continues its free-market reforms.

Three Elements of U.S.-Russian Cooperation

Where do the United States and Russia fit into this process? At the first hearing of the U.S. Senate Foreign Relations Committee in February 1992 on the START (Strategic Arms Reduction Talks) process, the committee asked whether past adversaries could cooperate and on what basis? What is in our mutual interest? Three areas of cooperation came out of those discussions.

The first is our military interest. It is centrally important to us and the world that the threat of conflict be reduced through arms cuts and that the defense budget cuts are prudent.

Second, in an era of Russian-American cooperation, threats around the world have changed. Consider some of the changes: the unification of Germany; the revolutions in Eastern Europe; the negotiations in the Middle East; the Cambodian settlement in Southeast Asia; changes in Cuba and Latin America. The reasons for both powers developing global systems of defense bases have now largely disappeared. In the late 1950s Nikita Khrushchev said, "We are now a global power and every issue in every region will be influenced by us." He was right. Every place where Russians and Americans had foreign involvements we both started out by asking what the other side was doing; that was a major reason for our military and diplomatic commitments. Today, there is great potential savings and improved prospects for peace from working cooperatively.

Third, we have mutual economic interests. Michael Camdessus, head of the International Monetary Fund, has developed two scenarios. In the optimistic scenario, Russia and the other republics, with Western support, are growing 4 percent a year by the turn of the century. This positive growth would increase world national product annually by about a half a percent or about $20 billion.

That growth could well be the difference between global prosperity and depression. The pessimistic scenario envisions a continuing decline of 20 to 30 percent in the region's output with the recession in the region primarily from the collapse of the market of the former Soviet Union.

But more specifically, the critical element that led to the U.S. House's support of the Freedom Support Act last summer was Majority Leader Gephardt's argument that we should "help Russia to help ourselves." If we invest in oil and help develop the Russian oil industry, this will create exports, profits, and jobs in this country. If we participate in telecommunications development, this will bring very substantial investment returns and employment to the United States. One can go through a series of industries where we can benefit. Why is this relevant to defense conversion? Because that's where the assets, expertise, and potential are for conversion and for developing profitable global commerce and reduced threats. Again these mutual interests are compelling:

• In assisting their reduction in military capabilities, we benefit from reduction in our defense spending, letting us transfer resources to other productive uses;

• In assisting in the dismantling of a confrontational, military-based foreign policy, we benefit from a cooperative international system under rule of law;

• In assisting in successful economic and political transformation, we help generate the market for profitable trade and investment and economic growth that can be translated into jobs and income.

The gravest threat is that we fail to take advantage of this historic opportunity. Failure could set in motion a long sequence of events where Russia, Ukraine, and much of this region may be lost to the community of democratic, market-oriented states.

Summit Charter Needs Implementation

The United States and Russia have a special relationship with opportunities and responsibilities on both sides for the development of an interactive, coordinated strategy. The need to develop such an approach was at the heart of the Charter for American-Russian Partnership and Friendship signed at the June Washington Summit. Of special and mutual interest would be an early, bilateral downscaling of forces and a reorientation and weapon dismantlement plan; a detailed global cooperative plan for building confidence, reducing tensions, and resolving international issues; a comprehensive foreign trade and investment plan to protect and assure maximum benefit for each side by creating an investment friendly reciprocal environment.

Direct involvement by top leaders would be required to bring this about. Only the former adversaries could effectively construct this comprehensive (security, political, and economic) system. If the charter were made operational it could then be the model for East-West transition toward peace and prosperity. It would be based on mutual interests in reducing defense expenditures and global tensions and in promoting trade and investment.

Mutual, Cooperative Arms Reduction Programs. The willingness of both sides to discuss frankly their short- and long-term military objectives will, to a large extent, determine the success of arms reduction. To live up to the spirit of the Charter, both sides should develop and share five-year force development and budget plans based on ratified arms reduction agreements. An American-Russian program for defense build-down could spell out a strategy for conversion and target American monetary and technical assistance to facilitate this restructuring. This cooperation could build confidence in the mutual process of reducing military capabilities.

In many ways, downscaling is even more daunting than upscaling, because we both must rechannel resources and, in many cases, destroy weapons. We have $400 million in the current budget to destroy weapons, but we don't know if there are other equally serious problems and bottlenecks. We fear that some unemployed scientists are liable to go to Baghdad or some other place endangering world peace; on an ad hoc basis, we then say we should take care of the scientists. Wouldn't it be much more reasonable to develop government-to-government agreements to deal in a coordinated, comprehensive way with such concerns?

Cooperative Foreign Policy to Reduce Global Tensions. We need bipartisan government-to-government agreements not only on downscaling military-based, confrontational foreign policies but also in upscaling the cooperation in the international arena. A cooperative foreign policy program could deal in an orderly way with many international issues, such as nuclear proliferation, arms sales, terrorism, and drugs as well as regional areas of tension. We must link, not separate, military and economic issues.

For example, we are leaving many countries the option of selling arms in order to balance their payments—not just Russia, but Brazil and a number of other countries. We must have an orderly plan to support our common interests and to focus and target our assistance and multilateral resources toward reducing international tensions and increasing the prospects for global peace and the rule of law.

Trade and Investment Strategy Needed to Promote Exports and Growth. The Charter for American-Russian Partnership and Freedom calls for the removal of barriers and promotion of trade and investment between Russia and the United States. Specifically, the charter states that Russia intends to speed up privatization and demonopolization, introduce structural and sectoral reform, and create policies directed at furthering competition and effective property and contract rights.

The Russian Federation intends to improve its laws in the fields of taxation, property, and contract law and those relating to intellectual property rights. The parties intend to lower constraints to trade and investment and to remove Cold War-era restrictions on business. As indicated in the Charter, the parties will also work to strengthen national export control systems, to prevent arms proliferation, and to promote high-technology trade and investment. America and Russia intend to work together bilaterally and multilaterally, particularly through the new COCOM (Coordinating Committee on Multilateral Export Controls) Cooperation Forum.

These are necessary, but not sufficient, steps to implement a trade and investment strategy. For example, the United States has tended to move slowly on critical issues, such as Russia's concerns about the slow pace of eliminating COCOM's high-technology restrictions. COCOM is no longer as restrictive as it once was. We should now be moving forward and looking at our trading relationship as mutually advantageous. Safeguard systems that we have in military programs can provide access to civilian enterprises and verify the use of dual-use technologies.

We should be urging Russian and U.S. government officials at the highest levels to facilitate major new investment and commercial agreements with private enterprises. The development of oil projects like the Kazakhstan-Chevron agreement to develop the Tengiz field may serve as a model. We need joint productivity committees headed by private-sector representatives to emulate the successful productivity and restructuring programs of the Marshall Plan. Productivity increases can be mutually beneficial and lead to foreign investment.

The United States also needs more facilitating mechanisms, including credit guarantee facilities and commerce-promoting legislation. Much of the U.S. legislation was passed during the Cold War when the Soviet planned economy assured a closed economy. The United States has recently begun to identify some legislation that impedes trade and investment but has not revised the legislative framework to conform to a policy of partnership and friendship in trade and investment.

Finally, Russia's unprecedented transformation of a command economy to a market economy in a democratic, not authoritarian, context will require broad domestic support and visionary and effective leadership. It will also require a near-term program that emphasizes restructuring, defense conversion, and an improved quality of life. In the long term, this transformation presents the possibility of a much more peaceful and productive world. A rising Russian economy will raise all boats, including our own.

In the West, we must act prudently and in our own self-interest. We must understand that defense conversion is not a side issue to be dealt with later, but a central issue that must be promptly addressed collectively as well as individually. If we fail to provide timely coordinated assistance, the crisis surrounding Yeltsin's reforms may deepen and lead to the collapse of order and the reforms of the Russian economy. A cooperative effort on defense conversion would be the greatest single contribution both sides could make to achieve global peace and prosperity. ⌞

2

Prospects for Russian-American Business Cooperation in Defense Conversion

Aleksei K. Ponomarev

Russian-American relations are entering a new era with the end of military confrontation — a confrontation where concentrating resources on the military sector clearly cost both countries dearly. Spinoffs from military research and development cannot compensate, especially in Russia, for lost opportunities in civilian production.

In Russia, demilitarizing the economy will be particularly difficult since conversion must occur during two types of fundamental systemic change: transition from a centralized to a market economy and an overall restructuring and decentralization of the economy.

While the first attempts at conversion have encountered many problems, cooperation in reducing our enormous military complexes can clearly be mutually beneficial to Russian and American companies and spur economic growth in both countries.

The Failure of the First Attempts at Joint Ventures

In 1990-91, American and Russian companies, especially companies in the defense sectors, began exploring business opportunities in earnest. Both countries, however, generally view these contacts as failures.

Russian participants cite the following principal problems:

1. American companies were frightened off by the uncertain direction of economic reforms and the lack of real progress in restructuring the Soviet economy.

2. American companies doubted the reliability of Russian partners and were concerned that many enterprises could not make good on their obligations to foreign companies.

3. Defense enterprises continued to be state owned and under the direct administrative control of government ministries. Practically all the

high-technology industries most attractive to foreign investors were part of the state-owned defense complex, and it was unclear if foreign firms could have any property rights.

4. Unrealistic ruble exchange rates and complicated exchange mechanisms made repatriation of profits very difficult.

5. Detailed laws to protect foreign investment were lacking.

6. The business infrastructure in Russia was inadequate. Information on defense enterprises was limited and poor.

A number of more subjective factors were equally important:

1. Both sides felt that negotiations often took place in different business languages. For example, Russian enterprise managers generally do not know how to present commercially viable business proposals or conduct market research.

2. Russian enterprise managers reacted suspiciously to the completely natural desire of American business people to establish legal guarantees for long-term joint projects.

3. American business people often complained that Russian enterprise managers were unwilling to consider new products.

4. The traditional assistance of specialized Russian "innovation," consulting, and intermediary firms in negotiations was completely ignored. This stemmed from both the incompetence and the small number of such Russian organizations, and American firms' limited understanding of operating conditions in Russia. In addition, Russian enterprise managers and ministerial leaders wanted to make decisions independently without sharing information.

American Barriers to Trade and Investment

There were also serious obstacles on the American side:

1. Many American business people felt that the U.S. Administration, particularly the Pentagon, retained a Cold War mentality and did not support increased economic cooperation. Large American companies, dependent on military orders, feared sanctions and lost contracts if they established close ties with the Russian defense industry.

2. There was no Russian-American trade agreement establishing a comprehensive framework for trade.

3. The U.S. Administration pursued a restrictive policy on technology exports through COCOM (Coordinating Committee on Multilateral Export Controls) and unilateral American export regulations.

4. There were no agreements, such as through the Overseas Protection Investment Corporation or the Russian government, to protect foreign

investment from political risks.

5. Most importantly, there seemed to be no clear desire on the part of the American political leadership to address these problems.

There were also important subjective factors on the American side:

1. American business people had a poor understanding of the economic and legal peculiarities of Russian enterprises.

2. Americans were unwilling to pursue non-traditional or complicated business plans.

3. A number of experienced American firms, accustomed to working with a central ministry, continued to rely on ministerial decisions long after that was necessary. They underestimated the increasing independence of enterprises from the ministries and the decreasing role of the government in industrial management.

4. Serious American entrepreneurs mistrusted the many Russian intermediaries and consulting firms, many of which were unscrupulous or incompetent.

Because of problems on both sides, by the end of 1991 or early 1992, American companies and Russian defense enterprises had largely stopped talking about joint projects. The record of Batterymarch, a leading American investment firm which had moved aggressively to seek defense conversion investments, is typical. The firm dropped its proposal for a defense conversion investment fund and did not carry out a single large-scale project. In essence, parties on both sides remained on the sidelines during the pre- and post-coup period, waiting for a more stable political and economic climate.

Investment Climate Changes in 1992

By the spring of 1992, the climate had begun to change. President Yeltsin's package of measures to liberalize foreign economic activity, government steps towards ruble convertibility, and the beginning of the privatization process were viewed by American business people as clear progress towards the creation of more normal business conditions. On the Russian side, decreased demand for high-tech products in the domestic market pushed Russian industrialists to more actively search for foreign partners.

There were also factors in the U.S. that led American industrialists to seek greater cooperation with Russian enterprises. By spring or early summer, America's economic troubles were becoming increasingly apparent, and large high-tech companies, dependent largely on Defense Department contracts, foresaw further defense budget cuts.

The curtailment of strategic weapons systems development in the

United States and the former Soviet Union has forced companies to rapidly diversify and to find new markets for their products. But entering new high-technology areas is too costly for many companies in this time of global recession. Moreover, Japan, Western Europe, and Southeast Asia are becoming increasingly competitive in high-technology markets. These factors are forcing American industrialists to turn to possible cooperation with the relatively inexpensive, high-technology sectors of the Russian economy.

Agreements reached at the June 1992 Summit lifted many of the U.S. Administration's restrictions on cooperation. Of particular importance was the agreement on defense conversion, which encourages cooperation with Russia's defense enterprises undergoing conversion. The agreement to protect foreign investment was yet another important step towards a better climate for investment.

This, of course, is far from full-blooded cooperation. Nevertheless, these are significant steps towards the establishment of a business infrastructure, the realization of mutually profitable projects, and the integration of Russia into the world economy.

Unquestionably, there are many unresolved problems. In particular, the U.S. government continues to strongly resist lifting COCOM restrictions and easing U.S. export controls. Large firms are still not ready to negotiate large-scale projects. Recently, however, small and medium-sized American companies have begun to focus on establishing close ties with larger industrial enterprises. These firms are looking for long-term opportunities and are working closely with American manufacturing firms.

An analysis of the activities of foreign firms in Russia shows that they most commonly strive towards minimal commercial risk by developing and commercializing intermediate technologies created by Russian enterprises. Once they are profitable, they begin to expand cooperation.

A possible variation could be for Russian enterprises to work as subcontractors to American firms to assemble foreign-made components for eventual re-export.

Another variation could be projects to assemble components, utilizing American technologies, for subsequent sale on the Russian market or export to third countries.

Recommendations for Foreign Firms Interested in Russia

Attempts to pinpoint one or two "golden technologies" from the vast spectrum of Russian science and technology have generally ended in failure. Russians have a number of databases, but most don't contain enough information for even a preliminary evaluation of a specific technology. In many spheres of science and technology, there can be much duplication and overlap among research institutes.

Moreover, Russian specialists are mistrustful of foreign companies that endlessly look for the right deal but never sign a contract. Therefore, it is extremely important that an American firm make painstaking preparations prior to a trip to Russia:

1. This preparation should include developing a list of American companies and their specific technology interests. This assessment speeds the search for a Russian partner.

2. Before making contacts in specific areas, the American firm should analyze its Russian counterparts using the knowledge and experience of Russian specialists in scientific and industrial policy. Those experts can evaluate the reliability and technical level of enterprises and laboratories.

3. A reliable and competent Russian partner is extremely important. The partner must be capable of working quickly and effectively in selecting potential projects. American companies make wide use of "protocol firms" that make hotel and transportation arrangements. That, however, is not enough. American firms should also plan well in advance to connect with an organization that can competently select projects on a given theme, make preliminary evaluations, and prepare all necessary information and contacts. Experience shows that the effective work of Russian specialists in these early stages, given the limited information on Russian enterprises and parlous economic situation, is critical.

4. Experience also shows that direct contacts at public conferences or during official negotiations at the executive level are useful for information exchange, but they don't always lead to full mutual understanding of proposed joint activities. Negotiating parties often begin to view each other as competitors, complicating the search for compromises.

Russian managers poorly understand foreign economic activities and world markets, which further complicates negotiations. Similarly, Americans poorly understand the opportunities in Russia and the legal and economic conditions of Russian enterprises.

Corporate managers must enter into negotiations thoroughly prepared and be willing to work cooperatively to develop creative solutions. The infrastructure for complicated investment projects is still in a formative stage, but it is not a barrier to most joint projects.

5. American firms should be aware that ministries no longer play the key role in approving joint projects. In the past, several ministries could simultaneously declare their jurisdiction over foreign investment projects. Current Russian legislation permits the vast majority of enterprises to establish direct contacts with foreign partners. The process of registering agreements

is not controlled and not complicated. Facilitating direct contacts between Russian enterprises and foreign companies is one of the main goals of Russia's foreign economic policy. Russian enterprise managers, however, don't always realize their level of independence from ministries.

6. American companies still face serious problems in obtaining adequate financial and operating information about Russian enterprises. This is caused, in part, by new private organizations that have sprung up in place of disbanded Soviet ministries. These organizations often attempt to monopolize information for their own benefit.

This lack of information also stems from enterprise managers' poor understanding of the need to disseminate complete information about their firm to potential investors. The Government and enterprises now understand the need to provide detailed information about investment opportunities. We believe that the recommendations in the Charter for American-Russian Partnership and Friendship, signed at the Bush-Yeltsin Summit in June, are a major step forward. We are attempting to improve the availability of information on Russia, particularly with the help of the U.S Department of Commerce's new program, the Business Information Service for the New Independent States (BISNIS).

7. Given the radical structural reforms taking place in the Russian economy, foreign partners must constantly monitor legislative and policy changes and the status of economic reforms. Research and analyses done under the aegis of the Russian government, by organizations such as the Interdepartmental Analytical Center, can help provide answers to these questions.

We hope that this can be a watershed time in Russian-American economic relations. Cooperative solutions to the problems of defense conversion are essential if we are to create new opportunities for Russian and American industry.

3

Russian Foreign Economic Policy and Defense Conversion

Sergei Y. Glaziev

The major goal of Russia's foreign economic policy is to assist and support the development and competitiveness of Russian enterprises by creating the necessary conditions for opening and integrating the economy into the international market. This is based on our belief that increased economic ties between Russia and the rest of the world will help to ensure that our present economic reforms are irreversible and successful. The Ministry of Foreign Economic Relations' role is to establish the conditions for opening the economy and to facilitate the exports of goods from the Russian military-industrial complex.

The Russian economy has been highly militarized over the past 70 years, so conversion of defense enterprises is a necessary and integral part of our overall economic liberalization progress. Consequently, overall economic conversion and defense conversion go hand in hand. An open economy can be achieved only through successful defense conversion. Otherwise, a strong civilian industry will not be developed and will not survive. If the Russian economy remains closed and if defense enterprises are not converted to civilian enterprises, these enterprises will continue to put pressure on the government to subsidize their production and put up new import barriers to protect themselves from foreign competition. Such a course would lead to economic stagnation.

On the other hand, defense conversion can occur only if there is an open Russian economy. Russian defense enterprises need to be able to compete and sell their products in the international market to obtain hard currency for conversion. They also need foreign investment and foreign partners to assist in the process of conversion. Since these enterprises have experienced a severe drop in Russian government military expenditures, experienced a severe drop in Russian government military expenditures, they need to find alternative markets for their products. The domestic market must also be developed.

However, alternative markets have not been developed to any great extent. Exports from the defense sector have not increased substantially during 1992 for a number of reasons. First, these enterprises do not have much experience in the international market. They lack the knowledge and experience needed to identify export products and market them. They lack information on whom to contact and how to negotiate such export deals.

Second, defense enterprises lack the financial resources to develop and carry out export strategies. There is no infrastructure available to provide credits or other financial assistance to facilitate exports.

Third, barriers to increased exports from Russia continue to exist in the West. These include the continuation of COCOM regulations as well as specific U.S. laws that limit the imports of certain Russian technologies. For example, although Russia is competitive in specific space technologies, foreign regulations do not allow Russian defense enterprises to sell these technologies abroad.

New Export Controls Needed on Military Technology

The Russian government understands the necessity of export controls to ensure that military technology is not widely distributed, particularly to unstable Third World countries. But at the same time, it is clear that the present COCOM export control regime does not stop the spread of dangerous weaponry. Instead, a new system of global export controls is needed which would satisfy the needs of all interested governments with high technologies. While the COCOM control list was revised in September 1991 and again in June 1992, these revisions represent only a gradual evolution of its policy and not a more fundamental reassessment of its goals. Our aim is to establish a collective security system with respect to export controls. To this end, the Russian government is presently establishing its own system of export controls that meets the requirements of COCOM.

With the signing of the Joint Russian-U.S. Declaration on Defense Conversion (June 1992), both Russia and the United States support the establishment of the COCOM Cooperation Forum on Export Control. This forum intends to "advance conversion through helping to remove barriers to high-technology trade, assisting in the establishment of COCOM-comparable export control regimes in Russia and the other new independent states, and establishing procedures to ensure the civilian end-use of sensitive goods and technologies on matters of common concern."

"Both parties agree that this process is based on their mutual determination to adhere strictly to world standards of export controls in the area of the nonproliferation of weapons of mass destruction and related technologies, missiles and missile technology, destabilizing conventional armaments, and dual-use goods and technologies." Russia was invited to participate in the COCOM Cooperation Forum meeting in November 1992 to discuss these issues, and it has also applied to join COCOM.

The Russian government has also removed its own import barriers. During the first half of 1992, Russia was probably the most liberal country in the world with respect to imports. No tariffs or quotas existed which would limit imports. Beginning in July 1992, the government imposed a temporary import tariff of 15 percent. The Supreme Soviet is expected to adopt a custom tariffs code by the end of 1992, so Russian import regulations will be similar to world practice.

As discussed above, both internal and external constraints hinder the ability of Russian defense enterprises to convert successfully. These include the absence of the necessary infrastructure in Russia, the lack of knowledge, experience, and information at the enterprise level, and the presence of foreign barriers to increased Russian exports. The Russian and American governments need to work together to identify and remove these constraints.

We do not count on U.S. government financial support for conversion of our defense industry. Rather, financial support should come from the private sector based on the commercial viability of the particular project. The role of both governments is to establish the overall framework and to help remove the obstacles to increased commercial relations between Russian and American firms. The newly established joint Defense Conversion Subcommittee represents a very timely and important organ which can help fulfill this role. It can further facilitate the exchange of information and help to establish further official bilateral agreements and projects on defense conversion, which is a very important issue for the Ministry of Foreign Economic Relations.   ▚

4

Economic Reform Strategies and the Problems of Conversion

Ivan S. Materov

Economic reforms in Russia are gaining strength. The year 1992 marks the final turning point toward a market economy. Market mechanisms are beginning to work. Radical economic reforms are happening. Widespread industrial privatization is beginning.

Economic reforms have three main elements: creation of a stable financial system; denationalization; and structural perestroika. These three elements are beginning to work together, creating a real base for the long-term rebirth of the country.

Defense conversion plays a major role in the economic reform process. As a result of traditional diversification, defense enterprises already play a significant role in supplying consumer goods in addition to their role of contributing to the military strength of the country. Enterprises in the defense sector currently account for almost one-fifth of all civilian manufacture of machines and more than one-fourth of non-food consumer goods (excluding light industry).

Defense conversion plays a particularly important role in the structural reform of Russia's industry. The influence of conversion has been felt noticeably over the last several years but has increased sharply since the beginning of the new economic reform program in 1992.

In 1991, consumer goods accounted for 60 percent of the defense sector's output, compared to 40 percent in 1988. In 1992, procurement of weapons and military equipment dropped sharply. As a result, defense enterprises reduced their military-based production to just 28 percent of their total output in the first half of 1992.

The overall decline of Russian industry as a whole has, of course, also affected the defense sector. During the early attempts at conversion from

1988 to 1990, production of consumer goods increased by an average of 6 percent annually. Since 1991, however, there has been a decline in the production of consumer goods. The decline in the production of consumer goods is considerably less in the defense sector than in industry as a whole.

In 1992, defense enterprises undergoing conversion experienced declines in output mainly in equipment for food processing, light industry, trade, and public catering (by 15 to 27 percent), and also in consumer appliances (by 12 to 27 percent). This decline was largely caused by payment problems that had not been completely resolved at the time of price liberalization and reforms in foreign trade and investment.

Effective demand for household appliances also fell. Average personal income in June of 1992 was 3.4 times higher than at the end of 1991. Prices on appliances, however, grew much faster. Televisions, for example, increased in price by 700 percent. Refrigerators increased in price by 1,800 percent.

Under such conditions, it is expected that in 1992 there will be a temporary decline in the production of certain types of household appliances compared to 1991. For example, production of refrigerators, washing machines, televisions, and tape recorders will be only 80 to 85 percent of 1991 levels. Production of radios, vacuum cleaners, and motorcycles will be 86 to 90 percent of 1991 levels. Production of VCRs, sewing machines, and other items, however, is increasing.

Defense enterprises, which have unused capacity, are increasing their production of modern equipment for oil extraction and refining. While traditional manufacturers are experiencing decreased production, defense enterprises undergoing conversion have increased output of equipment for the oil industry by as much as 800 percent. Potential domestic demand is high due to high equipment wear.

The Role of the Russian Government

The Russian government views the conversion of the defense sector as one of the key elements of future industrial growth.

There will, of course, be ongoing efforts to revitalize individual sectors of the economy. We expect to concentrate capital in the agro-industrial complex in coming years. Gradually, as the standard of living increases, and the economic situation stabilizes, we expect increased investment in residential construction.

In addition to traditionally effective investment in the export of raw materials, investment will become important in the development of technologies for resource conservation. The Russian government is ready to discuss various measures to attract both domestic and foreign capital to this sector.

The potential domestic demand for transportation and communications infrastructure is also great. Both government and rapidly developing, nongovernment trade structures have an interest in the rapid development of this sector. Russia will continue to develop industries such as aviation and shipbuilding that are capable, to a large extent, of satisfying domestic demand while having considerable export potential.

The government believes that in all the areas stated above the conversion of the defense sector could become the core of restructuring and the base for industrial growth. We are opening the possibility for the participation of foreign capital in enterprises undergoing not only 100 percent conversion, but also in those retaining a portion of their military production. It must be noted that the process of incorporation, begun in the second half of 1992, will affect most defense enterprises.

Protecting foreign investment and creating favorable conditions for joint ventures is, at the present time, a high priority for the government. Foreign partners are important for us not only as a source of additional investment in industry, but also as a stimulus for institutional reforms, including privatization and new legal and organizational forms of enterprise functioning.

Current Russian legislation permits direct contacts between foreign and Russian enterprises, including enterprises of the defense sector. Government structures have been called upon to provide all possible support for mutually beneficial cooperation.

We hope that the Russian-American Defense Conversion Subcommittee, chaired jointly by representatives from the U.S. Department of Commerce and the Russian Ministry of Economics and Finance, will help break down barriers to cooperation with Russia's defense enterprises undergoing conversion.

II

The View from the Ministries

P art Two presents the viewpoints on defense conversion of a select group of Russian policymakers at the national and regional levels. These articles illustrate the difficulties faced by the government in developing a comprehensive coordinated strategy toward conversion. They point out that conversion is extremely complex due to its linkages to other critical political, military, economic, and social issues. An overview of these issues, which are discussed more fully in the following articles, is presented below.

Russian Defense Conversion Policy and Strategies

Political/Military Concerns. A number of Russian ministers explain that it is difficult to plan for conversion when the political situation is unstable, and the new military doctrine and related defense force structure are not yet in place. The Russian government announced in April 1992 that it intends to decrease its military troops to 1.2 to 1.3 million from 2.5 to 3 million, and adopt a defensive military posture. Since that time, the Russian Ministries of Defense and Economy have prepared the government's military procurement orders for 1993, which are approximately at the same level as in 1992, according to Deputy Minister of the Economy Ivan Materov. A longer-term military strategy, which will include multi-year defense expenditures, is still being developed.

Given the rapid decreases in the Russian defense budget, President Yeltsin and his government have been under strong pressure from defense-related enterprises to allow them to increase their sales of weapons and other military equipment. Many Russian defense plant managers complain that U.S. defense companies have been able to increase their arms sales worldwide as a result of the drop in arms sales from Russia and the other former Soviet republics. (Note: U.S. annual arms exports have increased from $11 billion in 1989 to $24.1 billion as of October 1992, while FSU arms sales have dropped from $15 billion in 1989 to $4 billion in 1991. Russian ministry officials and the U.S. Central Intelligence Agency state that arms production decreased 85 percent in 1992 in the FSU, which has led to an even bigger drop in arms exports.)

The deteriorating financial condition of defense enterprises has increased the pressure on the Russian government to allow arms exports, at the same time as the United States government objects to many of these sales. For example, one Russian company, Glavkosmos, is selling a rocket booster to India. Other Russian enterprises have been given permission by the government to sell diesel submarines to Iran, and missile-guidance technology, rocket engines, and other advanced weapons systems to China.

Support of Enterprise Managers Is Critical

While these weapons sales could lead to increased tensions between Russia and the United States, the Russian government also needs the support of its military sector, particularly the managers of defense-related enterprises. These individuals are capable of influencing the government's political processes and products, acting through the Union of Industrialists led by Arkady Volsky.

Volsky's group advocates a stronger state hand in the management of economic reform and a slower transition toward an open market. The Russian League of Defense Enterprises has called for a more interventionist industrial policy that would determine which enterprises should be converted and which military technology capabilities should be preserved. Pressures such as these led to the appointment of a new Prime Minister Victor Chernomyrdin and the dismissal of Acting Prime Minister Yegor Gaidar in December 1992.

Sergei Glaziev, the new Minister of Foreign Economic Relations, has previously stated that the "opening of the military-industrial complex and the high-technology sector is the key to conversion in Russia. It will be difficult to achieve this without foreign participation. But the opening of this complex is important politically, because once it is opened, it will end the totalitarian regime forever."

Ministry officials therefore argue that fending off political pressures from the military-industrial complex is a major reason for providing greater assistance for Russian defense conversion. One leading official confessed that the government wants money for conversion in order to distribute these funds to defense enterprises so as to ensure their continued political support. But these funds are also needed to help finance conversion. What is not clear is if the two purposes can be made to coincide and whether the earnings from arms sales are being used to help finance conversion.

Economic Issues. Defense conversion is viewed as an integral component of Russia's overall economic reform program. However, the Russian Administration and Parliament still do not agree on the scope and pace of either economic reforms or of conversion. According to Evgenii Rogovskii, director of the Department of Export Strategy, Ministry of Foreign Economic Relations, "while everyone is giving lip service to conversion in Russia, there is a lack of understanding that it must be based on a sound economic framework and that it must be commercially attractive in order to succeed."

Conversion is closely related to the processes of privatization and ownership of defense-related enterprises. On August 18, 1992, President Yeltsin announced the government's privatization program, which went into effect on October 1, 1992. Every Russian citizen has received a voucher worth 10,000 rubles (approximately $66, or four months' average salary) to participate in the purchase of state-owned assets. If citizens do not want to use these vouchers to buy shares in state-owned companies, they may sell them to banks for investment certificates or to other Russians for cash.

The government has plans to privatize small industrial enterprises and most of the housing stock by 1994. Agriculture and farm land, notably, are exempt. The government's goal is to privatize 50 to 60 percent of state-owned industries by the end of 1995. Large defense enterprises are to be included starting in early 1993. The process will be an extended one, starting with the transformation of these enterprises into state-owned joint stock companies and then proceeding to the sale and distribution of shares to certificate holders.

One of the biggest obstacles to defense conversion is the unavailability of transitional financing. It is estimated that conversion will initially affect 800 to 1,000 defense enterprises and about one million to five million people in Russia. What is not clear is how much this effort will cost and how these costs will be paid. State Counselor on Conversion Malei declared at a NATO Cooperation Seminar in May 1992 that Russian conversion will take 15 years and cost $150 billion. This figure has been disputed by other Russian officials as being too high.

Five major revenue sources were identified by Russian ministry officials and defense enterprise managers: arms sales; exports of major resources, such as oil, minerals, and timber; international assistance; foreign investment; and government financial assistance. An examination of these five sources reveals that there is no single panacea for supplying the necessary capital to carry out conversion. Instead, a number of approaches may have to be combined to amass the resources necessary to meet the conversion challenge.

Social Issues. Directly related to the lack of financing is the issue of rising unemployment within the Russian military-industrial complex. The latest official unemployment statistics (from November 1992) show that unemployment is still less than one million, although this figure is regarded as too low, because millions of people are still officially on the payrolls but are not being paid.

Most defense enterprises are no longer financially viable. In fact, it is estimated that it would cost approximately one trillion rubles per month to keep all such enterprises afloat. Massive social programs are not now in place to meet the rising unemployment, and the government is also faced with the possibilities of increased social unrest and strikes as more and more defense plants will have to close.

The problem of unemployment is the responsibility of the Russian Ministry of Labor, which is presently considering various alternatives. One plan that is being discussed is a broad public works program to be financed by the Russian government, although where the money for this program would come from is unstated.

The Ministry of Defense is also being challenged on this front. The army is currently decreasing more slowly in size than the GNP, according to Materov. Therefore, the Ministry needs to find funds for salaries, pensions, housing, clothing, transportation, and other costs for the soldiers.

The papers that follow demonstrate that traditional definitions of conversion do not fit the current Russian situation. Within the government, conversion has been viewed first in political and military terms, and then in economic and social terms. Based on discussions at the seminar, the participants have redefined conversion as a means of adding economic value and employment within the Russian economy.

The perspectives and roles of the major ministries and departments on conversion are included here. This includes the Office of Deputy Prime Minister Khizha, and the Ministries of Defense, Foreign Affairs, Foreign Economic Relations, and Science.

In addition, the paper by Valerian M. Sobolev, first deputy head of the Volgograd Regional Administration, emphasizes the need for a stronger regional role in conversion. He presents the model that is being developed in the Volgograd Region to support conversion.   ↳

5

Defense Conversion: Problems and Solutions

Andrei O. Gorbachev

S uccessful defense conversion is one of the greatest challenges facing Russia in this transitional period. Most defense enterprises have lost state defense orders and sources of financing, and require colossal expenditures for conversion. These problems do much to deepen the economic crisis in Russia. The benefits of defense conversion will be felt in the economy only after 2 or 3 years, when military productive capacities are converted to civilian production. Defense conversion not only does not reduce the budget deficit, it also places an additional burden on the economy. For each ruble saved on reduced military procurements, one ruble and 20 kopecks must be spent on defense conversion.

At first, decisions on cutting military production were made without adequate preparation at the enterprise level, priorities for utilizing released resources, or mechanisms to stimulate civilian production. State orders for weapons and military equipment for 1993 are being sent to enterprises despite the absence of a completed military doctrine. These orders are at the same level as 1992's orders, which was a decrease of over 75 percent. Without a coherent military doctrine, there can be no clear picture of future weaponry and military equipment needs or a strategy for weapons export.

Nevertheless, recent experience with defense conversion is useful, because it shows the scale of the problem and underlines the need for tremendous efforts by enterprise personnel and the government. Past experience also underscores the necessity of developing effective forms of international cooperation in the area of defense conversion.

Defense Conversion and the State

In 1992, more than 550 defense enterprises in 89 regions of Russia are subject to conversion. As a result of significant cuts in military production, more and more defense plants are becoming unprofitable. These enterprises will need financial support from the government during conversion.

In 1992, most of the expenses required for refitting factories, reconstruction, and establishing civilian production lines are being covered in the form of favorable credits provided by the government to the Central Bank. This credit is available to enterprises and organizations focusing on civilian production in specific priority areas identified by the government. The enterprises must have concrete business plans guaranteeing repayment by 1996. The identified priority areas include energy, transportation and communications, agriculture, medicine, chemicals and timber, and the environment.

Given very severe budget constraints, government conversion policy sets criteria for state support. The criteria include: one of the priority areas listed above; consumer goods for which there is a guaranteed long-term market, export potential, or the potential to replace current imports.

Favorable credit is now the only economic device available to facilitate conversion. To date, 527 conversion programs have already been confirmed, and another 300 are still being developed.

Defense Conversion and the Region

In addition to focusing on specific industrial sectors, defense conversion strategy also has a regional focus. The government is developing zones for conversion through the following steps:

• Forming regional non-budgetary assistance funds for conversion in the form of a 50-percent reduction in the tax and payment burden of defense enterprises in the targeted regions;

• Agreements between the Ministry of Economics and regional administrations to provide tax credits for conversion programs for 1992-96.

•Transferring to the regional level expenses for the maintenance and development of the social infrastructure of enterprises of the defense and atomic sectors.

Legislation is now being developed to financially support enterprises undergoing conversion. This legislation is in the form of amendments to the Russian law on taxation. The amendments would give defense enterprises exemptions for reinvesting profits into conversion. This includes the government decree of December 24, 1991, which permits ministries to create non-budgetary funds for research and development and new high-technology product development. The source of these funds is a 3 percent tax on goods produced by defense enterprises.

A study of 50 large defense enterprises, conducted by the Ministry of

Economy, shows that there is a real threat of losing many advanced technologies developed in the defense sector for weapons and military equipment. These technologies are rocket technology and space-based weapons systems, military equipment with modern radio-electronic capabilities, and optical-electronic systems and equipment.

These technologies become lost when enterprises lack the means or the external budgetary support to preserve high-tech productive capacities. Experts believe that released productive capacities and technologies should be redirected toward high-quality civilian production, including civilian aviation and marine equipment; space systems for navigation and environmental monitoring; the location and extraction of natural resources; medical equipment; and technologically advanced household appliances.

Defense conversion and the establishment of market relations require an effective mechanism for adapting technologies and designs, formerly used for military purposes, to civilian uses. These mechanisms could include incentives for acquiring and developing "dual-use" technologies for widespread application in the civilian economy.

The state can only guarantee the prerequisites for defense conversion, adequate availability of information and financial support. But the real process of conversion takes place at the micro, regional and enterprise level.

Thus, the prospects for finding new uses for released military assets depend on the enterprises developing conversion programs. By introducing competition under very tight financial restrictions, the enterprises must fight for attention, change their mental outlook, and develop products that meet high consumer demands. They must reduce production expenses and the time it takes to begin production (to meet repayment schedules to commercial banks). In other works, enterprises must act independently to increase efficiency at the micro level.

Defense Conversion and the Market

With the progress of economic reforms, the center of gravity is shifting to the implementation of conversion at the regional level. This requires creating market structures (regional center, associations, funds, etc.) to help attract financing, especially financing from the non-government sector and from foreign investors. These structures will also help to develop horizontal ties at the regional level.

To carry out conversion at the regional and local levels, the appropriate policy framework must be established by the central government. This includes laws and regulations related to the denationalization and privatization of state defense enterprises. Denationalization of these enterprises is important given their high level of monopolization; their vertical and horizontal interrelationships throughout the former Soviet Union; their previous high levels of secrecy; and the need to maintain some defense capabilities.

The government is developing its future military force requirements and defense mobilization plans. These plans will determine what enterprises can be converted quickly and those that must remain 100 percent military or continue to produce for both the military and civilian markets (i.e., dual-use industries). There is a need to preserve some state defense enterprises based on state priorities for research, weapons development and strategic parity. Therefore, this policy is still evolving.

Defense enterprises undergoing 100 percent conversion to civilian output will be privatized according to existing legislation. Most defense enterprises can now be restructured into joint-stock companies, with part of the stock owned by the state and part owned by the managers and employees, as well as by foreign investors.

With respect to foreign investment in these enterprises, there must be a well-developed policy to protect foreign investment and create favorable conditions for international cooperation. These policies are also being considered.

Establishing an appropriate framework and regulations will require the joint efforts of the state and entrepreneurs, both Russian and foreign. The government's role should be to coordinate regional cooperation and provide necessary information. Experts believe that such an approach will create favorable conditions for entrepreneurship and, at the same time, take into account regional interests and circumstances.

Despite the difficulties in the defense sector and the economy as a whole, the government and the enterprises agree on the problems of conversion. There is recognition that there must be widespread support for conversion activities. Support includes appropriate legislation, a system of incentives, and favorable conditions for the privatization of defense enterprises that includes Russian and foreign entrepreneurs.

Achieving international cooperation in the area of defense conversion will require that regional administrations respond positively to foreign initiatives. Cooperation can be grounded in the interests of Western governments, especially the United States, to help create a smaller, more stable, and precisely defined defense complex in Russia.

6

Western Involvement in Defense Conversion

Sergei G. Chevardov

S oviet defense enterprises operated for decades under strict rules of secrecy that blocked practically all serious contacts with foreign entrepreneurs. As a result, the best part of Soviet industry remained out of the field of view of potential foreign investors and partners. This situation has begun to change rapidly in recent years.

Russian defense enterprises and research and development organizations possess hundreds of thousands of technologies, many of which still have not found commercial applications. Research conducted by the Center for Conversion and Privatization of the Institute for the Study of the USA and Canada (ISKAN) has shown that developers of new technologies, both in the defense enterprises and in institutes of the former USSR Academy of Sciences, made use of ample freedom in selecting areas of research. In the interest of developing the former Soviet Union's defense potential, they were generously funded and they could carry out exploratory research in nearly any field without taking into consideration any specific final application for the new technology.

This situation has now changed. Russian defense enterprises, research institutes, and other organizations are actively seeking foreign partners to assist them in identifying and commercializing the most viable technologies. These organizations are also seeking to establish joint research and development firms with foreign partners that utilize Russian engineers and scientists. Such joint ventures could develop specific components under contract with foreign firms or with combined Russian and foreign capital.

While exploring and developing joint ventures to commercialize Russian technologies, it is also desirable for the Russian government to develop policies that protect the country's scientific potential. Such a policy should support the capabilities of the best research staffs and engineering schools in Russia.

Industrial Opportunities for Foreign Firms

There are several forms of cooperation between Russian and foreign partners in the area of manufacturing:

• Creation of non-defense production within defense enterprises to assemble goods primarily for export. In the interests of Russian industry, agreements with foreign partners should include the opportunity to gradually replace imported components with components produced in Russia, as is customary in many other countries.

• The manufacture of goods designed and assembled primarily in Russia, but fitted with imported parts and components. This category includes, for example, airplanes designed in Russia but equipped with foreign-made engines and electronics.

• The manufacture of components based on orders by foreign firms.

• The manufacture of finished goods based on foreign licenses with a significant number of the components produced in Russia.

A priority area for attracting foreign investment into Russia's converting defense industry is the energy sector. Foreign investment could be used to develop Russia's enormous energy resources. Russian enterprises, government ministries, and foreign companies should, to the maximum extent possible, include Russian defense sector enterprises in major oil and gas extraction projects, and refinery or petrochemical plant construction and modernization. Defense enterprises could produce a significant amount of the equipment for oil and gas extraction, transportation, refining, and petrochemical processing. Part of this equipment could also be exported.

Government studies, conducted by ISKAN's Center for Conversion and Privatization, indicate that this kind of equipment production can be accomplished on a large scale and in a relatively short period by factories that build ships, rockets, tanks, and artillery. One advantage is the low cost of labor in Russia, which will remain low for at least 15 to 20 years. This can significantly reduce costs for Russian and foreign partners in developing new oil and gas fields in Russia.

Such projects should be supported by both the Russian and foreign governments. Right now one the foremost projects is the large-scale development of the Shtokmakovskii gas field (one of the largest in the world) located in the Barents Sea. Shipyards in the city of Severodvinsk that formerly built strategic nuclear submarines could be used. Those shipyards currently employ more than 200,000 people.

Russia's Foreign Investment and Industrial Policies

Russia's policy for attracting foreign investment in industry should be based on Russia's national industrial policy, which has yet to be formulated. The experiences of Japan, Germany, Italy, and South Korea could be useful for the government to consider.

Russia has made significant scientific and technological achievements which could be used to make a number of Russian products internationally competitive, especially if Russian enterprises make use of strategic alliances with foreign partners. Considering the huge potential domestic market of Russia and other CIS member states, it would be counterproductive, however, to formulate a policy that encourages only export-oriented manufacturing. In each case, there should be commercially justified proportions established between goods produced for the domestic market and for export.

7

Technology Transfer and Conversion

Boris D. Yurlov

Reorienting Russia's scientific and industrial export potential is one of the main strategies for economic growth in times of sharply declining domestic demand for high-technology products. Government policy on technology transfer plays a major role in foreign affairs and in domestic economic development. It also influences economic, scientific, military, and cultural cooperation among countries.

The main goal of Russia's policy on technology transfer is to create and develop a legal and administrative system to protect the interests of those involved in technology transfer. The government is now developing domestic and foreign policies that consider national interests and security. In the process of developing domestic and foreign policies on technology transfer, the following goals must be considered:

First, the central goal of government policy is to stimulate structural changes and the export of high-technology products. Stimuli include:

• Industrial restructuring programs aimed at increasing the export competitiveness of high-tech products.

• Favorable credit lines for export.

• Tax incentives to reinvest profits in new production.

• Active steps in the foreign policy arena to remove foreign barriers to Russian high-technology exports.

• The creation of an export credit and insurance infrastructure.

A second, and no less important, goal is to create conditions that permit the transfer and assimilation of advanced foreign technologies by Russian enterprises. This can be accomplished by:

• Establishment of government subsidies for importing new technologies.

• Encouragement of multinational corporations to invest in the Russian defense sector.

• Efforts to remove political barriers against the export of technology and capital to Russia.

• Encouragement of foreign governments to support private-sector cooperation with Russian enterprises.

Third, Russia cannot become effectively integrated into world markets without government efforts to protect the interests of Russian high-technology industries in both domestic and world markets. Efforts to remove foreign barriers against Russian exports must be accompanied by corresponding internal measures, such as:

• Creation of a market for high-tech goods and services (this includes creating a patent and licensing system, exchanging scientific information, protecting intellectual and industrial property, and adopting international standards).

• Creation of a system of favorable credit and partial subsidies for high-technology exports designed to provide temporary protection against foreign competitors on Russia's domestic markets.

• Creation of an infrastructure for effective horizontal ties within Russian industry. An effective infrastructure includes all-Russian databases and information networks and regional centers for interdisciplinary research and technology transfer. A special state "Agency for Technology Transfer" should be established to assist interregional, cross-sectoral, and international technology transfer.

Fourth, expenditures should be minimized on projects in which Russia cannot play a leading role and which are not likely to contribute to economic growth in the near future. To facilitate Russia's entry into the international scientific and technological community in coming years, it is necessary to:

• Create internationally acceptable legal, economic, and administrative conditions for enterprises and individuals taking part in international technical cooperation.

• Bring Russia's internal legislation on scientific activities in line with international norms and initiate on that basis regular consultations, information exchanges, and ongoing cooperation with foreign countries.

The specific goals of Russia's technology transfer policy should be to:

• Protect the rights of and stimulate the activities of high-technology producers and consumers.

- Protect national security interests in the transfer of technology.
- Improve the scientific, technological, economic, and military potential of the country through active assimilation of new technologies and information on research and development.
- Increase the competitiveness of domestic producers in internal and external markets by intensifying and utilizing technology transfer.

Government Should Support, Not Manage, Transfer

The government, however, cannot directly manage the technology transfer process. It lacks the highly qualified specialists that are needed to carry this out. Government management also would serve to complicate relations among parties to technology transfer. Therefore, holders of intellectual property and intermediary firms must be empowered to take part in the technology transfer process directly, with the role of the state limited to regulatory and support functions.

Government support functions include creating a system of laws designed to normalize technology transfer processes. During the first half of 1992, the President and the Government have adopted nearly two dozen laws and measures that now comprise the legislative basis of foreign economic activity. In particular, the Russian president's decree "On the Liberalization of Foreign Economic Activity on the Territory of the RSFSR" gave all enterprises the right for the first time to engage in import-export operations. Four laws have been adopted to regulate property rights during technology transfer: a patent law, a law on trademarks, a law on legal protections for computer programs and databases, and a law protecting microchip designs. A draft of the Russian Federation law "On Measures to Stimulate International Assistance to Russia's Pure Sciences" has been prepared. That law will grant tax incentives to projects funded by international grants.

In addition to establishing the policy and other favorable conditions for technology transfer, the government can assist by providing information on defense enterprises and technologies. Government regulations on the level and type of information that can be provided must be based on the continuing need to protect national interests; limit abuse in technology transfer, such as disadvantageous transactions that harm the state; and stop any financial misappropriations.

Currently, legal regulations remain inadequate in nearly every sphere of technology transfer. This is true not only in Russia. Nevertheless, Russia, using internationally accepted norms, is systematically working towards the establishment of a legal system that adheres to international conventions. That work is still far from complete. One of the major problems requiring immediate action is the legal definition of types of intellectual property. The extremely low prices for intellectual property, resulting from state control of price-setting mechanisms, very negatively affects Russia's scientific community.

Legislative measures are being taken to overcome these problems. Chapter IX of the Russian Federation law "On the Conversion of the Defense Industry of the Russian Federation" establishes the right of enterprises to independently exchange technology, licenses, know-how, and scientific information. The mechanisms for transferring intellectual property, however, are still incomplete.

The new system of patent law assumes a specific patentee, thus resolving uncertainties about the ownership of an invention. There remain, however, unresolved issues regarding author's certificates on ownership of inventions.

Legal System Must Guarantee Innovator's Rights

Given the monopoly of state enterprises and an underdeveloped system of innovation firms, individual patents do not lead to technological innovations, since state enterprises do not have adequate stimuli for innovation, and patentees do not have adequate opportunities to implement their designs. The innovation process is very risky and requires large capital and labor investments. An owner of capital must have a vested interest in the outcome of the process. That vested interest can only exist if there is a legal system to guarantee rights to a particular innovation.

The result of an innovation is a concrete good, technology, or process representing a certain type of intellectual property that must belong to the developer. The developer (or distributor) must have rights to all the results of the innovation.

The most difficult problem is how to acquire ownership of intellectual property that has been developed prior to the current legislation. That problem can be partially solved by exchanging USSR author's certificates for patents and the issuing of appropriate licenses to enterprises that have utilized the intellectual property.

World experience shows that legal measures can only discourage, but not completely eliminate, illegal commercial use of intellectual property. The most important aspect in protecting the rights of an owner of intellectual property is not so much regulatory measures, but rather the opportunity and readiness to beat competitors in the race to produce and market a final product. Here an extremely important aspect is the establishment of measures to prevent technology drain during the development and marketing process. These measures must be based on very carefully developed personnel policies within government structures and private firms. Policies should provide economic, social, and psychological motivations for the behavior of inventors and all those involved in the technology transfer process.

As laws based on internationally accepted norms are introduced in Russia and other CIS members, it is possible that past violations of the rights of foreign technology owners will be discovered. Such violations were previously hidden by the secret nature of the work. To a large extent, this may also be due to the limited resources of government ministries and patent agencies and limited knowledge of Western practices.

These reasons do not, however, absolve those involved in technology transfer from any legal responsibility for violating the rights of intellectual property owners. Therefore, in the technology transfer process it is possible that third parties can dispute an individual's or enterprise's right to intellectual and industrial property. U.S. firms that are engaged in the buying, leasing, or commercializing of Russian technologies should be aware of who has the rights to this asset. While the laws on ownership are not yet fully developed, it is important to ascertain whether the particular individual, enterprise, or other entity has the right to sell or lease the technology. Consequently, there is without question a need to create a state system to protect the interests of foreign intellectual property owners. On the other hand, there must also be both a voluntary choice of that protection and rightful reward for the protection.

Defense Conversion and Exports

Increasing the export potential of defense enterprises undergoing conversion plays an important role in Russia's foreign economic policy. An active foreign policy directed at attracting foreign investment, removing discriminatory barriers to Russian exports, and promoting the economic interests of Russia is vital to reorienting the Russian defense sector toward the world market.

Russia's access to world markets is now inhibited by artificial barriers created by the members of NATO. These barriers include the COCOM (Coordinating Committee on Multilateral Export Controls) list of forbidden technologies, unfavorable trade restrictions, and outright discrimination against Russia on high-technology markets. Overcoming these barriers and promoting the competitiveness of Russian high-technology goods is vital to recovering from the current economic crisis and for overall long-term economic growth.

Keep in mind that the scientific and technological potential of the former Soviet Union was primarily intended for military purposes. The technologies available in the defense sector are those that are most attractive for transfer both domestically and abroad. Of all the republics of the former Soviet Union, Russia has the highest concentration of defense-oriented R&D facilities. The former USSR and the United States were the only countries that conducted research in nearly every field. In many cases, Soviet technologies were competitive with — or even superior to — technologies developed abroad.

However, the secrecy surrounding many of those technologies presents transfer problems. Many technologies suitable for transfer, because they are connected with other classified technologies, require special documentation to be declassified. This documentation is particularly difficult given the absence of clear laws, a developed financial system, qualified personnel, and market capabilities.

These problems become even more significant when technology is being transferred to foreign countries. Foreign interest in Russian technologies is not just of a commercial nature. It also includes a desire to obtain information about Russia's scientific research, military strength and development, and strategies and potential in world markets. Moreover, in the international technology transfer process there is a risk of a "brain drain" from Russia.

Most technologies available in the Russian defense sector have undergone very little commercial development due to the past isolation and secretive nature of that sector. The problems of defense sector technology transfer are all the more serious in the context of privatization. There is a threat of dissemination of technologies outside Russia by former co-developers and by the illegal actions of individuals not bound by loyalty to the rightful owner of the technologies.

Many technologies that are now ready to be transferred were once considered state secrets. Inadequate control over technology transfer could have negative short- and long-term consequences for national security. There is no set of criteria to judge the possible loss resulting from transfer of technologies vital to Russia's security interests. There is now a problem with deteriorating confidentiality, a problem that could harm both the state and the rightful owners of intellectual property. Foreign technology transfer control is now based on two presidential decrees, "On Measures to

Establish a System of Export Control in Russia" and "On Export Control for Nuclear Materials, Equipment, and Technologies." The Russian Ministry of Economy is presently preparing a list of technologies forbidden for export.

Widespread technology transfer, along with scientific cooperation in general, is clearly in the interest of the state. It increases the wealth of the country by increasing the wealth of technology owners and by increasing tax revenues. It also strengthens international relations and helps limit "brain drain."

An analysis of the real situation in the sphere of technology transfer reveals not only real flaws, but also gives us an opportunity to formulate goals and suggestions for technology transfer strategy. These include:

1. The government must support the technology transfer process by providing long-term credit for export-oriented industries.

2. The government should help create joint companies, such as holding companies that have potentially transferrable technologies. A network of joint ventures should be established to utilize concrete technologies and produce high-technology goods, as well as a network of joint marketing firms. The government should invest in large Russian projects and encourage the participation of Russian companies in high-technology production abroad.

The primary strategy for cooperation on technology transfer should include private initiatives, a focus on specific regions, and appropriate government support. Without government support and assistance, it is unlikely that Russian enterprises — particularly defense enterprises — will be able to enter the world market quickly or on a large scale.

High-Technology Exports and Economic Restructuring

Evgenii A. Rogovskii

Based on the Program for Deepening Economic Reforms for the period until 1995-96, the Russian Federation Government views defense conversion as one of the priorities in its structural policy during the present stage of economic reforms in Russia. This policy of structural perestroika should include the demilitarization of the economy, the return of ineffectively utilized resources to the economic cycle, and the formation of a new national export base. The government has established a goal of enacting an active, targeted strategy to facilitate structural reforms. While that strategy should not disrupt the establishment of market relations, it does involve managing the restructuring process in the interest of supporting social and political security.

One of the keys to economic reform in Russia is the conversion of defense enterprises, which are the most technologically advanced industries. Consequently, one of the primary questions with which we are grappling is, "What is necessary to make defense enterprises the leaders or 'locomotives' for economic restructuring in Russia?"

To answer this question, we must first focus on the concepts of stabilization and subsequent economic growth, which should be based on effective demand and realistic opportunities for investment. Demand and investment opportunities primarily exist abroad. Therefore, the Russian economy must adapt to the world market. This conclusion determines our foreign economic priorities, the logic and doctrine of our foreign economic relations, and the nature of the corresponding institutional changes required to bring about economic reform.

If we want Russia's exports to equal Russia's status as a great power and guarantee Russia's place in the international economic system, then we must substantially modify Russia's export structure to emphasize the export of high-technology manufactured goods and services. We must reverse the uncontrolled export of strategic raw materials and the import of foreign-made goods. In other words, we must capitalize income from exports and mobilize other financial sources and investments for the targeted state support of export-oriented, high-technology products.

Foreign Economic Priorities

Russia's medium-term, foreign economic priorities are based on the following principles:

1. Export for the sake of more exports. More precisely, the capitalization of income from raw materials export should be used to develop the country's export potential. Initially, the main goal of capitalization should be to support traditional export industries. At the same time, large-scale service exports should be developed such as freight, international transportation services (ship repair, truck maintenance, navigational guidance flights), environmental services, research in the field of physics, computer programming. Later, non-traditional export areas should be emphasized such as Russia's high value-added technologies and unique spheres of knowledge. This knowledge is currently being sold wholesale at extremely low prices, especially in the fields of materials sciences, geology, and merchant marine development.

New export priorities are connected with Russia's initiative to execute a number of global projects. The United Nations and other international organizations are experiencing a shortage of resources. There is a possibility of providing goods and services to those organizations at sharply reduced prices rather than increasing Russia's membership dues. Thus, Russia could increase its exports by providing international organizations with high-technology services in fields such as equipment utilization, the environment, and medicine.

2. Regional technological integration with foreign partners. One of the main elements of Russia's foreign economy policy is to link regional export development programs. An important aspect of this includes establishing programs to maximize the utilization of defense sector resources in regional defense conversion programs. This could be carried out in regions such as Uralskii, Povolzhskii, Volgo-Vyatskii, Severo-Zapadnyi, Tsentral'no-Chernozemnyi, Uzhno-Evropeiskii, and Zapadno-Sibirskii.

Regional export development and defense conversion efforts should be carried out in close cooperation with central management organs and develop information about the most attractive defense sector opportunities for domestic and foreign investment. This information could include proposals to optimize cooperation and marketing under new or existing national and international export development programs.

This kind of cooperation has already begun in a number of regions. Foreign entrepreneurs have already expressed interest in these activities, and they are ready to help in the evaluation of defense enterprise capabilities and the marketing of defense sector products on a regional level.

3. Support for transregional and transnational corporations. The implementation of large-scale technological projects could serve as the basis for reconstructing economic ties within the framework of interregional and international cooperation. Russia's biggest economic problem is the disruption of existing ties among traditional partners. This disruption was caused by the collapse of central planning and the command-administrative nature of previous economic ties. The vertical association of enterprises — from raw materials and manufacturing to sale of the final product — with a focus on specific markets and consumers will permit the reestablishment of lost ties with former Comecon and other foreign partners on a substantially new basis.

There is, however, the grave danger that certain foreign partners could use Russia as a dumping ground for potentially dangerous activities, such as manufacturing processes that use atomic energy or radioactive materials, and environmentally unsafe resource extraction. Therefore, there should be an independent mechanism to safeguard against potentially dangerous projects. There is also a need to provide environmental safeguards as a part of any commercial project.

Defense Conversion Strategy

Support for defense conversion is an integral part of Russia's economic reforms. According to government strategy, the main goals of defense conversion at the present time include:

1. Preserving the most valuable elements of the manufacturing, personnel, and R&D potential of the defense sector.

2. Utilizing these elements to raise the technological level of civilian production;

3. Developing an export base and import-replacing production while reducing military production to the minimal level required to guarantee national security in new geopolitical and strategic conditions.

The process of defense conversion is not an isolated program within Russia's medium and long-term economic strategies. Rather, conversion is a multifaceted scheme that must be carefully conceived and developed.

Unfortunately, there is no organization within Russia or abroad that fully comprehends what is necessary to convert defense enterprises. No one can comprehend the entire chain of reactions that will be set off by massive restructuring and conversion of enterprises within the Russian economy.

We do, however, understand some of the prerequisites for carrying out conversion. These include the development of the necessary infrastructure, financing mechanisms, and information. It is impossible to develop joint ventures to commercialize technologies within the defense sector without an infrastructure that supports these projects. This includes the appropriate macro- and microeconomic frameworks, including laws and regulations, as well as the availability of communications and transportation networks, and other support services.

Financing is also a key ingredient in the ability to convert a defense enterprise to civilian production. Countries with market economies have different types of financial mechanisms and institutions, including the role of venture capital, to assist in this process. Russia has nothing of the sort. Therefore, we would like to attract foreign partners who can provide these services.

In addition, there is a lack of information on business-related opportunities with defense enterprises, including their potentials for conversion. Much of this information has been unavailable due to past conditions of secrecy under the guise of national security. We understand that past and current restrictions on the freedom and availability of information on defense enterprises has nothing to do with actual national security concerns. Real national security interests, including economic interests, have been substituted by irresponsible ministerial controls over the availability of information, excessive secrecy, and chronic distortions of economic and technological information.

This situation hinders the establishment of new cooperative relationships among producers within Russia and with foreign partners, which leads to large-scale miscalculations in investment and technology policies. The absence of a regulated system for information exchange also leads to major mistakes in foreign economic policy. The absence of a legal system that treats intellectual property like a commodity has resulted in major mistakes in foreign trade, such as drastically undervaluing scientific information. The Russian Federation Ministry of Foreign Economic Relations will provide informational support to foreign partners with the goal of conducting an information policy that is fair and mutually beneficial to all parties involved.

More and more large industrial and banking corporations, as well as an ever increasing number of small and mid-sized firms, are seeking to invest in the conversion of the Russian defense sector. The best opportunities for foreign firms are in applied research that commercializes for civilian use, both domestically and abroad, technologies developed in the defense sector. It is important to use existing defense technologies for new civilian applications. There are many technologies developed in the defense sector that could be used for civilian industry. Direct utilization of this potential is presently hindered by ministerial barriers and technological isolation. These barriers can best be overcome by using foreign capital to conduct joint development and marketing activities.

We believe that the best spheres for foreign cooperation include:

• Using the capabilities of the isotope industry for producing materials of high purity, especially for use in electronics (silicon, gallium, etc.) and optics.

• Using rocket technologies for high-tech chemical production.

• Using the machine-building capabilities of the atomic and space industries for chemical industry equipment.

• Marketing helicopters internationally.

• Using Russian designs and engineers to build civilian airplanes.

• Using composites, ceramics, and special alloys for engine construction and other purposes.

• Developing civilian applications for laser technology.

• Developing alternative energy sources.

We believe that government and private sector financing and technical assistance for defense conversion will create new forms of mutually beneficial cooperation between Russian and American partners. The Russian Ministry of Foreign Economic Relations is ready to assist U.S. firms in this critical endeavor.   ⌐

9

A Regional Approach to Conversion

Valerian M. Sobolev

The Volgograd region of Russia is actively promoting and pursuing conversion of defense enterprises located there. The regional authority to carry out conversion is based on the Law on Regional Administration and President Yeltsin's statements that Russian territories have both rights and responsibilities toward regional economic development.

However, the regional approach and mentality are so new in our country that we have not yet developed the proper conditions or mechanisms for successful, widespread reforms at this level. Consequently, we need to construct and implement sound regional strategies for conversion with assistance from the West in a variety of areas.

The Volgograd Regional Administration is developing a comprehensive program to support conversion that includes the following elements:

- Industrial restructuring.
- Agricultural restructuring.
- Creation of new financial institutions, such as the Southern Russian Bank to help finance innovative commercial projects.
- Social reforms, including some social safety net programs for workers that are laid off.
- Government financial support for concrete conversion projects, such as assistance to high-technology firms and to attract venture capital.
- Special programs to identify and support foreign investment in the region.

Once these programs are in place, the mechanisms for implementing them must include the participation of all relevant authorities, such as representatives from the banks, managers of defense enterprises, entrepreneurs, and appropriate government officials. As foreign firms become more involved in this process, their interests must also be represented.

One of the main difficulties facing enterprises undergoing conversion is insufficient capital. We are examining various ways to overcome this critical obstacle. For example, the oblast has control over resources in the region. It is possible that we could sell or lease the rights to develop these resources, including some strategic minerals, to foreign developers, and then use these funds to support conversion.

A second way is to attract foreign investment to commercialize high technologies that exist in our defense plants and that are based on our natural resource base. One such project that has already been carried out involves the use of magnesium oxide in medical technologies. We possess other commercially viable technologies, including superglass, complex rubber compounds that have a number of uses including aerospace technologies, and a new type of cold water washing machine, among others. We have a lot of know-how and innovation, but we lack the knowledge and experience to develop and market these technologies. Therefore, we are extremely interested in identifying and working with sound American and Western partners on mutually beneficial joint projects.

We are also working with the national government and will take part in any investment programs it develops to support conversion. With respect to broader government and enterprise support for conversion, there is a need for much greater interregional cooperation in Russia and throughout the former Soviet Union. We must work together; time is of the essence to develop and implement sound policies and programs to support conversion at the national, regional, and local levels.

10

Defense Conversion in Russia: The Need for Multilateral Support

Sergei V. Kortunov

Conversion of defense industries to civilian production is critical if Russia is to have a well-balanced, responsive economy. Without effective and timely conversion of defense industries, economic reform could fail. But if conversion is to succeed, the Russian government must dramatically reverse its policies; American companies must be encouraged to invest and their investments must be protected; and the U.S. government must change its restrictive Cold War policies.

Defense industries are capable of producing high-technology goods that equal or surpass world standards, but these industries have long operated under their own rules. Market-oriented economic reforms are now changing these rules and are a major problem for isolated and privileged defense industries.

Conversion and timid steps toward a market economy, for example, have sharply increased prices for civilian products manufactured by military factories, reduced living standards for this most skilled group of workers, and led to a disintegration of the system of state orders. Does that mean that defense industries and a market economy are entirely incompatible? Many people think so. Some believe defense industries are a major obstacle to market and economic reforms.

I believe this is a superficial view. The defense industries have monopolized the country's scientific, engineering, and labor elite, and have the potential to be a vital component of a market economy.

Shifting Economic Priorities Is Essential

Why is defense conversion so critical to economic reform in Russia? In the United States, defense spending accounts for only 5 percent of GNP. At the current and projected rate of the defense budget cuts (about 4 percent a year in real terms), cuts will only decrease the GNP about 0.2 percent a year. A reasonably healthy economy can easily bridge that gap with a moderate increases in industrial output. Therefore, the decline of U.S. defense spending is not a serious macroeconomic problem, even though it causes severe dislocation for some companies, employees, and communities.

The former Soviet Union has been spending more than 20 percent of its GNP on defense, which is one of the reasons for the country's deep economic crisis. To reduce spending to U.S. levels in a few years would decrease the GNP about 5 percent a year, or about 25 times the rate of decline in the United States. This would occur when the rest of the economy is in dramatic decline. As daunting as these figures may seem, they don't capture the entire problem, which is qualitative as well as quantitative.

The Russian defense industries have the highest quality of any industry in the country, the best engineers and managers, access to scarce materials, and a functional support infrastructure. Thus the American approach to defense spending, which lets market forces consolidate the industry, cannot be duplicated in Russia. Such a significant part of the Russian national economy cannot be permitted to vanish. Russia must use these resources to make products badly needed in the civilian economy.

Even more important, any fundamental and durable transformation of the security relationship between the United States and the former Soviet Union will tend to break the military-industrial complex's grip on national resources. This will promote a productive market economy and stable democratic institutions.

Defense conversion is more than restructuring old plants to produce civilian goods. Sometimes that will be feasible; often it won't. Rather, defense conversion is an integral part of a comprehensive post-Communist reform process requiring a massive shift in society's priorities and its ways of doing business. It will involve large-scale redeployment and retraining of manpower resources; systematic identification of facilities and enterprises that can be adapted and those that must be closed; elimination of barriers and creation of incentives for private-sector involvement; and development of a rational and accountable defense acquisition system. But above all, it will require that the democratically elected leaders of the new independent states make responsible tradeoffs between legitimate defense requirements and the economic and social needs of their people.

Since the Soviet defense industries competed with the military-industrial complex of the West, they had to meet world standards. It's no longer doubted that these defense industries employ manpower whose "commercial value" and skills match international standards.

It would be extremely undesirable, if not criminal, to dissipate this potential. And yet, there is a risk that this may happen in the current conversion program. Military factories are now stepping up consumer goods' output while still manufacturing their military products, instead of converting their facilities entirely to civilian production. Meanwhile, fundamental research, which depends on defense budget subsidies, has declined.

Defense conversion is difficult even when there is a well conceived program; unfortunately, the current program has failed to analyze the critical role and fate of military factories. This is understandable. The powerful administrative elite of the military-industrial complex has traditionally had its way. Their one-sided views are bound to be counterproductive and economically disadvantageous to the country as a whole.

While Russia and the United States have common problems in defense conversion, there is also a critical difference. The Russian military-industrial complex is state owned. The government simply does not have the resources to convert defense industries to civilian production. Therefore, the role of the Russian government must be to assist the private sector, especially in privatization and the formation of stock markets.

Finally, it must be frankly admitted that Russia needs outside help in the fundamental reform of its military-industrial complex and in developing these new nongovernmental organizations. Without such help and the integration of the Russian economy into the world economy, conversion is irrelevant and doomed to failure.

International Cooperation Is Essential for Conversion

Defense enterprises must be given more autonomy to alter their production. The state, however, can help with fundamental market research that helps converted enterprises gain access to world markets. The best way for enterprises to switch from military to civilian production is to become an integral part of major international projects, such as Eureka, the European civilian research program, the development of "electronic money," improvement of air traffic control in Russia, and the construction of high-speed railways. These cooperative ventures would provide access to Western economic, intellectual, and technological resources while commercializing advanced technologies developed by defense industries.

It should be noted, however, that attempts to establish business links with potential American partners have been irregular and unprofessional. There are a number of existing and new organizations, which are duplicating each other's efforts. In the process, they are misleading U.S. companies and raising doubts about the reliability and competence of Russian partners.

There has been an increasing number of cases where former employees of the military-industrial complex, presidents of various associations and foundations, have tried to set forth Russia's position on conversion without being authorized to do it. To clarify these issues and provide information to the business community abroad, the government has set up the Coordinating Council to be its liaison with governments and the business community abroad. This group is headed by Mikhail Malei, advisor to the president of the Russian Federation on matters of conversion, and includes representatives of the Ministry of Industry and the Ministry of Foreign Affairs. In the Ministry of Foreign Affairs, a special department has been established to deal with conversion and to assist the Russian and foreign business communities in developing contacts and organizing mutually beneficial projects.

The only official sources of information are Malei, his group, and authorized representatives of the Ministry of Industry and Ministry of Foreign Affairs. Considering the nationwide character of this activity, it should be supervised by a single government agency. While ensuring prompt political decision making, such an agency could be regarded by U.S. companies as a guarantor of commitments made by their Russian partners.

At the same time, a flexible and efficient conversion program requires direct contacts with the West on a non-governmental basis. It can be done within the framework of an independent association of enterprises. In other words, we need a mechanism for broad cooperation between Russia and foreign nations, a mechanism which combines governmental and nongovernmental arrangements. Western businessmen need to work with nongovernmental organizations that are initially supported by the state. There should be a network of information agencies, data banks, and consultants. Our long-term goal should be to create conditions so that enterprises can act independently or through nongovernmental organizations without government involvement.

In this connection, last July, the non-governmental, non-profit, Moscow-based Integration Association was registered and started operations. The Association unites Russia's leading defense enterprises and research institutions in their efforts to promote the integration of Russian high technology industries into the world market economy. The Association seeks to establish direct links between its members at home and abroad; identify promising areas and mutually beneficial joint projects and programs of international cooperation; utilize advanced technologies, know-how, production, and manpower potential in aerospace, nuclear, communications, transportation, and ecological fields; and help create a favorable environment for foreign investment in the Russian economy.

The organizational and operational concept of the Association was thoroughly discussed and widely supported at the International Conference on Russian Defense Industries' Conversion held under its aegis in Moscow this summer. More than 100 leaders of Russian major defense enterprises met with high-level representatives of more than 40 Western companies, legal firms and banks, as well as governmental and nongovernmental experts from Russia, Western Europe, the United States, and Canada.

The Association has established a good working relationship with governmental bodies of the Russian Federation, including Ministries of Foreign Affairs, Industry, Defense, Office of the Adviser to the President on Conversion Matters, and key committees of the Supreme Soviet. Preparations for organizing association branch offices in various industrial regions of Russia, such as the Volga Region (Nizhny Novgorod, Ulyanovsk), the Urals (Chelyabinsk), Northwestern Region (St. Petersburg) as well as in other CIS countries are being completed.

The quasi-official status of the Association can provide reliable access to the CIS military and industrial complex. In addition, the Association's network of contacts can facilitate, in some instances, the issuance by the U.S. administration of export licenses for sensitive technologies.

If Russian defense industries receive significant injections of Western capital to aid conversion, they will be encouraged to produce consumer goods for domestic and world markets rather than military goods. This would reduce the possibility of war and military conflict.

Target Government Conversion Aid

But Russian defense industries face a number of problems in converting to civilian production. They have had the luxury of being the most wasteful branch of the economy and have monopolized the best manpower and resources. The defense sector will now have to become an integral part of the market economy and even compete and bid for defense contracts. The Russian defense industries have a good chance to survive in this new domestic market environment and must use these new management skills to compete in international markets.

The Russian government can encourage and support defense conversion with the following measures:

1. Make public as soon as possible a national security policy and military doctrine (issued by the president or minister of defense) outlining the size and composition of armed forces and military capital/equipment require-

ments; cutbacks in defense industry production; priority areas of conversion. In addition, the government should formally invite international cooperation in conversion.

2. Make a presidential appeal to American business people, welcoming their energetic involvement in Russian defense industry conversion. The government must also provide specific information on the protection of private investments.

3. Make clear that many industries will be closed or cut drastically. Others will be restructured along market lines through personnel retraining programs, abandonment of old technologies, and introduction of new technologies with the help of foreign partners.

4. Undertake projects which use and preserve the most talented designer and management teams; set up these projects in new joint-stock enterprises, not in their current organizational structures. Encourage the establishment of limited partnerships, holding companies, and small ventures that would incorporate talented designers and engineers and encourage privatization of these new structures.

5. Arrange a fast track for projects which contribute to upgrading and developing infrastructure, such as transportation and telecommunication systems, for extracting and distributing energy, and for processing and distributing food.

6. Promote the establishment of joint ventures with American companies which can provide manufacturing, marketing, and financial skills necessary to succeed in the market.

7. Accelerate the privatization of defense enterprises by transferring state-owned assets needed for conversion to these newly formed stock-joint companies.

8. Accelerate the establishment of the legal and financial infrastructure necessary for companies doing business in a market economy and for forming business partnerships with American companies.

9. Ease the visa application process for business people involved in conversion projects.

10. Separate conversion projects from the existing defense plant and governmental bureaucracies. This separation should be accomplished by creating new stock enterprises or other business entities to develop, manufacture, and market new commercial products. Conversion projects would transfer appropriate personnel and would use existing facilities (obtaining new buildings is very difficult) of large defense companies.

These new entities should seek to form partnerships with U.S. companies in order to get immediate access to the capital, marketing, and management skills needed in a market economy.

11. Introduce tax exemptions for conversion projects and other long-term privileges and benefits for U.S. companies involved in such projects. The government should identify these measures as soon as possible.

12. Develop a national program of step-by-step disclosure of the defense industries' human, material, and scientific potential.

13. Establish a financial climate favorable to normal banking operations.

14. Adopt international standards related to the joint technological projects (e.g., civil aviation).

15. Promote sales of high technologies abroad through exhibitions, seminars, etc. Create joint projects to design, produce, and sell competitive high-tech goods. Comprehensive joint ventures are one of the best ways to generate needed hard currency and speed Russia's integration into the world economy.

Short- and Long-Term Aid from West Is Needed

If and when the government develops a viable defense conversion program, it will need, and I believe will receive, the backing of Western nations, especially the United States. Focusing defense conversion on development of infrastructure, for example, will delay the use of defense facilities for production of needed consumer goods. While development of infrastructure will promote an efficient consumer market in the long run, it will do nothing to alleviate the drastic shortage of consumer goods in the short run. Western nations must understand that structural economic reforms take time and that they should be prepared to buy time by providing humanitarian assistance, especially food and clothing, under generous credit terms.

The U.S. government must also support and encourage American companies involved in joint ventures in the defense sector. If American firms do not find attractive opportunities, no amount of government assistance will help. But there is a surprisingly large number of American companies seriously interested in creating joint ventures with Russian companies.

These partners recognize, and many of them have experienced, the problems of joint ventures with Russian companies: the lack of legal, financial, and communication infrastructure and the long-term commitment required for financial success. But as the new Russian government commits itself to real economic reform, American executives are finding a more attractive "risk/reward ratio."

U.S. Government Action Is Needed

American executives are looking for positive actions from the new Russian authorities and their government. I believe that Western governments, especially the U.S. government, should take the following inexpensive actions and that they should be endorsed at the highest political level:

1. Eliminate those COCOM (Coordinating Committee on Multilateral Export Controls) restraints on specific defense conversion programs. In practice, this would involve an approval procedure for joint ventures on defense conversion. The approval could require a waiver of restrictions when controlled components are needed. The product could be made and verified with appropriate end-use certification. The end-use should be relatively easy to verify, since American experts would be involved in manufacturing and marketing. For many in Russia, COCOM is a reminder of the Cold War and is a national putdown.

2. Provide technical assistance for the creation in Russia of the legal and financial infrastructure needed to compete in global markets. U.S. partners can provide some of this technical assistance, but the cost and volume of assistance exceeds private resources, especially when immediate profitability is unlikely. Public multilateral programs and subsidies will be needed.

3. Provide technical assistance to companies trying to form joint ventures in Russia. This would involve establishing information offices in Washington, London, Bonn, Paris, and other capitals, plus a few field offices in Russia. These offices should be staffed with people having business experience, especially in establishing joint ventures. They would be experts in the progress of economic reforms in Russia and understand how to conduct business in the evolving economic system. Retired executives fresh from business could be engaged in these field offices.

4. Create an Insurance Protection Corporation for American companies doing business in Russia (similar to the Overseas Private Investment Corporation) to protect businesses from failures resulting from major political changes after the joint venture is established. Beyond this, the U.S. government, with the participation of Russian experts, should study new forms of guarantees for foreign investors in Russia.

5. Expand existing exchanges and start them, if they do not exist, in each CIS state. These programs should include university-to-university exchanges and people-to-people programs, as well as programs that link professional groups such as military officers, lawyers, and scientists.

6. Give immediate consideration to eliminating or suspending legislative prohibitions, enacted during the Cold War, on trade and aid to Russia

and CIS states. This would include the Jackson-Vanik, Stevenson, Byrd, Church, and Johnson amendments, restrictions on Export-Import Bank credits, and ceilings on Overseas Private Investment Corporation coverage. Many of these restrictions have now been lifted.

7. Support the active involvement of the American private sector. In addition to reviewing outmoded legislative restrictions, private-sector involvement should be facilitated by streamlining export licensing procedures, updating the list of prohibited technologies, facilitating visa issuance for business visitors from Russia and other CIS countries, and working with each country to improve operating conditions for American business.

8. Provide macroeconomic assistance, such as stabilization funds for debt management, through existing international organizations. In this regard, the United States should provide their fair share of additional IMF special drawing rights and encourage vigorous IMF and World Bank involvement in the economic development of Russia and other CIS states, including both commercial and investment banking.

9. Facilitate the access of American companies to the technology base in Russia:

• Sponsor technology fairs for the benefit of American nondefense companies and technical agencies that showcase the technology of defence-sector companies and research institutes of Russia.

• Establish exchange agreements with Russian institutes and centers in the military-industrial enterprises to work on technologies for the American nondefense private sector.

10. Continue to provide humanitarian assistance under generous credit terms, especially food and clothing, until economic reforms take effect.

11. The government should also consider establishing low-interest loans for American companies involved in conversion projects. This move would be considerably more costly than those I have mentioned, and its necessity has yet to be determined. However, the U.S. government in supervising the defense conversion program should be mindful of instituting such a low-interest loan program at a later date.

Just as each American company considering a joint venture has to make a "risk/reward" assessment, so the U.S. government has to do the same before embarking on a program to assist Russia's defense conversion. Although the costs of the recommended programs are not high, they are not risk free. Balanced against those risks are the "rewards" that would attend successful defense conversion in Russia.

Some have argued that the real risk is that conversion will succeed, and that at some later date, Russians will reconvert these more efficient plants back to defense production. The real issue is not whether conversion or no conversion would provide a more efficient base for rearming, but which alternative would make this undesirable alternative less likely. I believe the incentives to rearm are much less likely under effective economic reform and a strong democratic government.

There is no serious basis for fearing that Russia will flood the world with arms in the near future. The arms market is divided, and it is very difficult to penetrate markets that have traditionally been supplied by the United States and its allies.

The Global Rewards of Successful Conversion

Whatever the "risks," the rewards of defense conversion far outweigh them.

1. Defense conversion is a critical ingredient in the overall program of the current economic reform in Russia. A total and extended collapse of the Russian economy makes the country vulnerable to: civil war, loss of control of nuclear weapons to irresponsible groups, and restoration of dictatorship.

2. Defense conversion reduces the routine resupply of large quantities of modern arms to the Russian military. It also reduces the level of arms exports to the Third World.

3. The defense conversion effort, particularly that part of it conducted through joint ventures, enhances the transparency of Russian defense activity. The whole process facilitates the verification of arms control treaties and reduces the need for Western countries to base their defense planning on "worst-case" estimates of Russian military capability.

4. Failure of defense conversion, along with stagnation in the Russian economy, would force the layoffs of large numbers of highly skilled weapons designers. There is the danger that some experts in nuclear weapons and ballistic missiles could end up working in covert Third World arms programs. The availability and spread of these world-class weapons engineers could substantially increase the proliferation of these weapons.

On balance, the American government should take reasonable steps to join Russia's conversion program. Let me underscore again, we don't expect Western governments to finance our defense conversion. Mr. Malei estimates the cost of conversion at $150 billion in the next several years. Neither our government or your government can afford this. We need your help in creating the legal, informational, economic and political infrastructure that will attract private investors. That is our joint task; the actions I have recommended would be quite effective and relatively low cost.

III.

The View from the Enterprises

T he articles in this section by two Russian defense enterprise managers, Vasilii P. Bakhar and Valerii V. Filippov, illustrate the difficulties in carrying out conversion at the enterprise level. Russian directors and managers often identify defense conversion with diversification. Plants appear to be pursuing different conversion strategies, with some of them producing the same product for the civilian market and some of them now involved in producing completely new and unrelated products. In discussions with these managers and other experts, five major issues were raised that affect Russian companies' capabilities to carry out conversion.

First, it is difficult for the managers to plan and implement conversion strategies at the enterprise level without greater policy guidance and assistance from the Russian government. This problem is particularly difficult for purely defense enterprises, whose managers have to decide whether and how much of their enterprises' capabilities can be converted to civilian production.

Defense plants have little or no opportunity to increase military production under the new government procurement policies. Many are still expected, however, to maintain some facilities and capabilities for military production until the government's long-term defense needs are determined, but this entails operating at a loss. Yet defense plant managers argue that they will not be able to shift back quickly, if at all, once their plants are fully converted to civilian production. This creates a dilemma that can be resolved only by governmental decisions that are themselves extremely difficult to make.

Second, there is a shortage of capital at the enterprise level to carry out conversion. This is one of the most serious obstacles to conversion, according to many Russian defense directors. As a consequence, most Russian managers would like to identify and work closely with American and/or other Western partners to develop and carry out specific conversion strategies. Foreign investment is also considered a critical ingredient to any successful conversion strategy.

These managers would also like their government to take a more active role in developing targeted assistance for specific conversion priorities; greater guarantees for foreign investment in conversion-related business projects; and more favorable tax rates and other incentives for enterprises choosing to convert to civilian production lines, among other possibilities.

Third, there is a lack of experience and know-how in retooling plants, redesigning productions, and retraining workers. Most of the plant managers said they need greater technical assistance in carrying out conversion. This includes training managers and retraining workers, reorganizing a plant's structure and design development, choosing new products, reequipping old plants, and developing and implementing a marketing strategy for the new products.

Spin Off Key Technologies

Fourth, there are social problems that inhibit an enterprise's ability to convert. Since most of these enterprises employ thousands of people, it is difficult to convert the entire enterprise. Most managers talk instead about identifying key technologies or products that can be spun off into newer, leaner enterprises with a chance of becoming commercially competitive. Yet, these managers also feel a responsibility for their employees, and many expressed concerns about the lack of other employment opportunities once a plant is shut down.

The issue of creating new jobs and retraining and reemploying workers within the military-industrial complex is addressed in this section by Sergei Kovalev and Aleksandr F. Kononenko from the Russian Federation Coordinating Council. This council is assisting defense enterprises to restructure and reorganize to create viable new companies that would provide employment to retrained military officers and defense workers.

Fifth, it is difficult to obtain U.S. high technology to assist in conversion and it is also difficult to export certain technologies to the United States. Quite a few plant managers reported that they have been engaged in concrete discussions with American firms concerning possible joint projects in high-technology fields. Two constraints that are holding back some of these projects are: 1) the continuation of U.S. export controls on the transfer to Russia of dual-use technologies; and 2) the inability to export certain Russian technologies to the United States.

The issue of U.S. export controls is being addressed through the "Joint Russian-U.S. Declaration on Defense Conversion" (June 1992). Both countries support the COCOM (Coordinating Committee for Multilateral Export Controls) Cooperation Forum on Export Control. This forum intends to "advance conversion through helping to remove barriers to high-technology trade, assisting in the establishment of COCOM-comparable export control regimes in Russia and the other new independent states, and establishing procedures to ensure the civil end-use of sensitive goods and technologies on matters of common concern. Both parties agree that this process is based on their mutual determination strictly to adhere to world standards of export controls in the area of the nonproliferation of weapons of mass destruction and related technologies, missiles and missile technology, destabilizing conventional armaments, and dual-use goods and technologies."

Russia was invited to participate in the COCOM Cooperation Forum meeting in November 1992 to discuss its adherence to COCOM regulations. Russia has also applied to join COCOM.

The COCOM Control List was significantly shortened in September 1991, although regulations still prohibited the export of basically all high-speed technologies. On June 1, 1992, COCOM agreed to liberalize significantly the export controls on telecommunications equipment to the FSU, effective July 1, 1992. However, a number of critical high technologies are still being controlled, and inconsistencies exist in the U.S. COCOM list. For example, the list restricts the export of computer chips but not the computers.

Export of High-Technology Goods Is Restricted

The inability to export certain high technologies from Russia to the United States is a problem in both countries. Russia is developing its own export control regime in order to stop the flow of certain critical high technologies to the West, and the United States still limits the importation of some technologies from Russia. This issue needs to be jointly addressed to facilitate greater involvement and cooperation between Russian and American business people.

Overall, Russian defense enterprise managers recognize the need to develop and carry out sound conversion strategies. One of their key questions is how they will be able to accomplish this given the absence of a sound macroeconomic framework and infrastructure, lack of capital, burgeoning unemployment, and other political, economic, and social issues that are also difficult to resolve. This section presents several different viewpoints from the Russian business trenches.

11

The Managers' Perspective:
Star Wars to High-Tech Consumer Goods

Vasilii P. Bakhar

The main business of Vympel was and is research and development into the production of anti-missile systems, early warning missile systems, and space control systems. It is still the major contractor of the defense ministry's strategic defense initiative.

Until late 1991, Vympel was 100 percent state owned; it existed as a conglomerate of scientific centers, design bureaus, manufacturing facilities, and construction enterprises located in Russia, Belarus, and Ukraine. It had more than 75,000 employees. In September 1992, these three governments transformed Vympel into a multinational open stockholding company. Presently, there are over 58,000 employees within Vympel; and a capital base of about 45 billion rubles at current prices. Vympel has been granted all property rights, including intellectual property rights. With the help of Western partners (the law firm Steptoe and Johnson and the consulting firm Booz, Allen & Hamilton), we are presently evaluating the commercial opportunities of the company.

My view of conversion differs from the perspectives of Russian government officials and other Russian defense enterprise managers because of the unique position of Vympel Corporation. The true definition of conversion — a complete reorientation from military to civilian production — does not accurately apply to Vympel. After a rapid decline in military orders two years ago, Vympel's military funding is now stable and even growing because of our high-technology expertise. But we believe that conversion is the only way to survive, which we define as diversification and the creation of high-technology spinoffs from our base of 25 years of experience in command, control, and communication systems.

Two Approaches to Conversion

Our first approach to conversion is to move from confrontation in defense to cooperation in strategic defense systems. This means that we are trying to internationalize Vympel's business activities in space control and early warning missile systems. We have proposed to the Russian and American governments that we establish an international early warning system for missile attacks. We understand that there are political problems involved in cooperating in this sphere, but we believe it is our mutual duty to persuade our governments to cooperate in this area. We are open to working with Western partners on this concept, and we are now financing this activity on our own.

Our second approach is conversion of our military technologies to civilian commercial uses. For example, we can use space control systems for control of pollution and fires, and even rescue at sea. With broad experience in radio electronics, the main direction of our conversion will be telecommunication systems. We have won the contract to be a general subcontractor for the a proposed Western-Russian global telecommunications system, and we are responsible for the ground-based segment. It will be based on the huge space platform that will be launched into orbit by the largest launcher in the world. This satellite communications system, Project North, will cover the northern part of the globe. We welcome foreign investors in this project.

Turning "Raw Diamonds" into Finished Jewels

During years of defense research and development we have come up with many distinguished discoveries, but they are considered "raw diamonds." We are aware of the technological threats to the United States from Japan, so we believe that the best way to meet these commercial challenges is by working together. In doing this, we can help each other become more internationally competitive.

There are advantages to U. S. firms that work with Russian defense enterprises such as Vympel. We have unique technologies and well-trained specialists. For example, we consider our software specialists to be the best in the world. American computers are far ahead of Russian computers, and to compete we must have much better software. We are now working on the architecture and software for the neural network computer systems where we believe we are a little bit ahead of the Japanese. Thus, it could be a good idea to join forces: our architecture, techniques, and software for the neural network computers with American microchip technology.

Moreover, we have developed a very specific technology for establishing reliable communication in plasma conditions (extreme atmospheric turbulence) that is of great importance for the U. S. shuttle and the Russian space program. We are in the final stage of developing technology to change the speed of radioactive decay. We can also use the software and hardware from military systems for global ecological monitoring with the addition of special sensors for pollution.

Obstacles to Conversion

We are producing unique equipment, but would like to move into mass production of consumer electronics, home appliances, and consumer goods using our manufacturing facilities under Western licenses. This aspect of conversion requires greater assistance from the West, particularly from Western businesses.

One of the major obstacles to conversion in Russia is the shortage of capital, particularly for investment in conversion products. In addition, we lack information, knowledge and experience on how to commercialize and market our high technologies. All of these issues can be addressed in cooperation with a sound foreign partner. We also need assistance in protecting the intellectual rights of our technologies, which requires the establishment of a sound government policy on this issue in cooperation with Western governments.

Export controls in the West and also in Russia are impeding or slowing the transfers of certain technologies that are needed for conversion of Russian defense enterprises. However, we believe that through joint development, we can overcome all of these obstacles and jointly market these high-technology products throughout the world.

Future Prospects

To overcome the shortage of capital for conversion, Vympel had been transferred into a holding company. We are now in the process of issuing stock. Twenty percent will belong to the government, around 15 percent to the employees and managers of the company, and 65 percent can be sold. The government will continue to control the parent company because of its importance in national security, so we are now establishing stockholding subsidiaries that are entirely civilian oriented. In some cases, we can even give control or a sizeable share to the Western partner.

We welcome any type of investment, from stock ownership in civilian-oriented subsidiaries to joint ventures. We have just established a joint-venture company in Russia for cellular telephone systems and services in Russia and the CIS. With an initial investment of approximately $2 - $2.5 million for a very small part of the company, we estimate that an investor can multiply his/her investment by seven times in one year. This is a very high rate of return. We are now ready to expand very rapidly in regions adjacent to Moscow and some areas in Volgograd.

The challenges to carrying out conversion at the enterprise level are great. While we are continuing to experience many difficulties, we have also made great strides in the past year. We look forward to working more closely with American firms in meeting these new challenges.   🌜

*Valerii V. Filippov*_____

The Scientific-Production Association "Ferrite" is a high-technology electronics enterprise based in St. Petersburg. We have been under the control of the famous "Nine" (the nine ministries controlling the defense industry of the former Soviet Union) and are unique in our combination of applied sciences and manufacturing of ferrite materials and components on the cutting edge of high technology. The enterprise specializes in microwave frequency instruments and magnetic ferrite recording heads for various applications including video equipment and computers.

In the nearly quarter of a century since its establishment in 1969, "Ferrite" has served as the Soviet equivalent of foreign firms such as TDK, Toshiba, LTT (France), Hughes, and General Dynamics. Now that it has become possible to publish data on Russian defense enterprises and to offer our own formerly secret goods on foreign markets, we find that our technologies, especially in the field of high-powered microwave instruments, are as good as or better than those developed in the West.

Our microwave components are distributed by the firm Dorado in Seattle, Washington and are competitive at a 1:1 ruble to dollar rate. A "Ferrite" instrument that sells for 1,000 rubles in Russia (roughly $3) sells for $1,000 on the world market. Because of the "wooden" ruble, brought about by erroneous economic policies in Russia, production of high-technology goods has become unprofitable today. Highly qualified specialists have to take extraordinary steps to sell products for a profit. Their only other alternative is to seek work in foreign countries, often for salaries that are extremely low by Western standards.

Obstacles to Conversion

On the policy side, our enterprises suffer from the lack of a clearly defined state policy on conversion and a complete military doctrine that can provide direction at the enterprise level. This absence of a clearly formulated military doctrine is a major problem at the microeconomic level; enterprises cannot proceed with strategic planning without a clear military doctrine. At the beginning of this year there were 109 government and private organizations involved in conversion and, for the most part, their activities were uncoordinated. Due to the confused state of defense conversion, many enterprise managers are acting independently and are using their technologies and highly qualified personnel to make new consumer goods. But we don't understand marketing and don't know how to work within a competitive framework. These factors plus the uncertainty of government credits, tax, and educational policy mean that most military industrial enterprises were on the verge of failure by the middle of the year.

In this crisis it is essential that we coordinate our efforts and discuss positive programs. In St. Petersburg, more than 30 enterprises and research institutes have gotten together, mostly from the military defense complex, to create the Association of Industrial Enterprises. SPA "Ferrite" consists of three divisions with a total of 5,500 employees. The lead division is a research institute employing 1,800 people including 100 specialists. Our output in 1992 will be 200 million rubles, 60 percent of which is in the form of pilot production of new products.

Ferrite owns a special design bureau. Ferromash employs 200 people and designs and produces in small quantities ferrite measuring instruments. Magma, the largest ferrite production facility in Russia, employs over 3,000 people and produces over 5,000 tons of ferrite per year.

Future Prospects

SPA "Ferrite" has been a state-owned enterprise, but in accordance with Yeltsin's decree and the current program to incorporate state enterprises, we will become an open joint stock company at the beginning of 1993. We hope to attract both domestic and foreign investments. A possible source of investment is V. Scherbakov's (former vice premier) privatization fund.

Our successful penetration of Western markets gives us a certain level of optimism as we restructure. The Dorado catalogue contains more than 300 ferrite components and devices produced by Ferrite. Our sales volume in 1992 will reach half a million dollars and could $15 million by 1995. More conservative projections put sales at somewhere around $5 million in 1995.

Part of "Ferrite's" export success stems from COCOM restrictions. They forced us to develop our own unique technologies and products that exceed Western levels. Falling trade barriers now give the West opportunities to buy our independently developed, cheaper, but high-quality products. Therefore, "Ferrite" has a very competitive position. We understand that we have to find and defend our niche in Western markets and are stockpiling goods in the U.S. worth over $400,000. Dorado and "Ferrite" are contributing to the development of technologies that would be impossible without microwave electronics.

Another opportunity for cooperation between the United States and Russia in the area of conversion could be joint collaboration on a giant supercollider. President Bush signed an agreement on this in early October. This project is worth over $10 billion dollars. In the President's words, this project will lead to the creation of a large number of jobs in his home state of Texas. The project will create jobs in St. Petersburg as well. "Ferrite" will play a major role in manufacturing ferrite materials for the supercollider.

This is important to us because Russia's civilian markets aren't yet ready to absorb products produced by the defense complex. The civilian sector has been starved for goods for so long that it has no taste for unique products. That is why it is so important that we have Western partners, who are more dynamic, willing to accept innovation, and believe in the high potential of the Russian defense complex.

Western investors must take the risk of working with Russian defense enterprises despite an unstable economic and political environment. In the end, the greatest risk occurs in the first six months, and he who starts first will be the first to get through the period of greatest uncertainty.   ⤶

12

Officer Retraining and Conversion

Sergei I. Kovalev and Aleksandr F. Kononenko

The Russian Coordinating Council approaches defense conversion from the perspective of creating jobs. We define conversion as the retraining and reemployment of millions of military and defense-related workers in civilian-related jobs. Our particular focus is the conversion of military officers; our council's goal is to create civilian work by the year 2000 for the approximately 100,000 military officers who will be discharged as a result of the proposed reduction in the Russian military. Finding work for mid-career military officers is especially critical as these officers could, if they are not retrained and reemployed, threaten the progress of Russian economic reform. In our surveys, 70 percent of these officers say they would like to become businessmen.

Our work involves two stages. In the first stage, we have identified a number of enterprises within the military-industrial complex that would like to be converted completely to civilian production. The larger defense enterprises will either expand their existing consumer goods production or move from defense production to civilian goods. The key to this conversion is privatization, a process essential in generating capital within Russia, in attracting Western investors, and in giving enterprises the flexibility to survive without state orders.

One of the necessary first steps on the path to conversion for these enterprises is to develop a privatization plan to create joint stock companies. This is important, because in order to move rapidly on conversion, small and medium-sized joint stock companies must be split off from the giant defense enterprises. We assist these enterprises to develop and implement a sound privatization strategy.

In the second stage, we help these enterprises develop a business plan that is related to their conversion and civilian production objectives and financing requirements. Western technical assistance can be most helpful in developing these business plans to attract outside investment. Foreign investment is viewed as a critical ingredient in this process.

As a part of these two efforts, the Council is developing training programs for officers to become managers of converted defense enterprises or to become proprietors of new small and mid-sized firms. These mid-level career military officers have received a good education in subjects such as engineering, electronics, mathematics, and other science-related issues. But they do not know how to adapt and apply this knowledge and their experiences to the new market realities. They do not understand in general how a market economy is structured or how a business operates within that environment. Therefore, their training must be appropriate to their needs and to the changing conditions in Russia. We are working with a select group of American partners to develop and implement a sound training program for these individuals based on their previous education, experience and skills, employment objectives, and market needs.

It is impossible to carry out conversion on a massive scale in Russia without paying greater emphasis and attention to employment and other social issues. The creation of new jobs and the retraining of millions of workers who will be dislocated as a result of the conversion process is critical. Our project is an integrated approach to this issue for one segment of the Russian population — military officers. Other such programs need to be developed and implemented at the national, regional and local levels. Conversion involves people. Unless this issue is urgently addressed, the conversion of massive Russian defense enterprises will fail.

IV.

The View from American Business

United States business, and particularly its defense industry, has much it can bring to the defense conversion process in Russia: managerial experience, technical know-how, an understanding of markets, and venture capital. This section presents two articles that examine the importance of U.S. business involvement in conversion-related business opportunities in Russia.

The first piece by Kathryn Wittneben is drawn from her recent study carried out for the American Committee on U.S.-CIS Relations at the request of the U.S. Department of State. This report, *American Business Involvement in Defense Conversion in the Former Soviet Union: Opportunities, Constraints, and Recommendations* (December 1992), was based on research and interviews with over 120 American, Russian, and Ukrainian government officials, business leaders, academics and other experts. Its purpose was to examine the opportunities and constraints affecting U.S. business involvement in defense conversion in the former Soviet Union (FSU), with a focus on Russia and Ukraine; and to present recommendations for what the U.S. Government can do to encourage American companies to take advantage of these opportunities. Three of the major findings from the study are:

• The United States will have to assume a more active leadership role in providing support and assistance for defense conversion in Russia.

• The American business community must become more actively involved in the defense conversion effort in Russia.

• The international community needs to develop a more concerted and supportive approach toward defense conversion in Russia.

Ms. Wittneben's article examines why U.S. companies are actively working with Russian defense enterprises and the obstacles they face.

Jeffrey Moore's piece is based on Grumman Corporation's attempts at conversion as well as its experiences in Russia. He argues that U.S. defense companies may have an advantage over nondefense industries in conversion-related work in Russia. Moreover, lessons gained from working with Russian defense enterprises on conversion-related projects can also be applied to conversion efforts in the United States. Mr. Moore examines some of these lessons, as well as several important issues that need to be addressed by both sides in developing mutually beneficial commercial projects.

13

Perspectives and the Role of U.S. Business in Russian Defense Conversion

Kathryn Wittneben

This paper presents an overview of U.S. business perspectives on working with Russian defense-related enterprises. It is drawn from interviews with over 100 U.S. business leaders, corporate representatives, and other experts who were asked the following questions:

• Is your company actively working with any Russian defense-related enterprises, and do any of these business activities or projects involve defense conversion? Why or why not is your company involved there?

• What are the opportunities for working with Russian defense-related enterprises? What are the opportunities for assisting in defense conversion?

• What are the constraints in working with Russian defense-related enterprises, and particularly on projects that involve or require defense conversion? Are these constraints based more on instabilities (political, economic, and social) in Russia; difficulties at the enterprise level in Russia; U.S. foreign economic policy; American business culture; or other factors?

In-depth answers to these questions were obtained from interviews conducted from mid-April to September 1992. The individuals who were interviewed came from a wide variety of U.S. industries that are currently examining or pursuing opportunities in Russia. Both defense- and nondefense-related industries were included: aerospace; electronics, tele-

This paper is adapted from Part Four of the report, American Business Involvement in Defense Conversion in the Former Soviet Union: Opportunities, Constraints, and Recommendations, *(December 1992) sponsored by the American Committee on US-CIS Relations. It is reprinted with permission from Margaret Chapman, project director, and Kathryn Wittneben, author.*

communications, and other high-technology industries (such as computer software); pharmaceutical; automotive and steel; machine tools; food processing; energy and environment; construction; transportation; and services, including investment banking and management/consulting. The private-sector individuals to be interviewed were selected by the American Committee trade director, with input from the U.S. Departments of State and Commerce and other industry experts.

The findings from these interviews show that a large number of U.S. companies are actively exploring opportunities in Russia, primarily with defense-related enterprises. This chapter surveys the reasons why U.S. firms are examining business opportunities with Russian defense plants; draws lessons from U.S. experiences working with these defense enterprises; and examines the constraints faced by American companies in conversion-related projects there. Specific projects are also presented.

Best Business Opportunities Are in Defense Industries

In general, U.S. corporate representatives stated that the best opportunities for U.S. business in Russia, as well as other former Soviet Union (FSU) republics such as Ukraine, are in their defense industries. Company representatives cited three major reasons why their companies are interested in working with Russian defense enterprises.

First, there is an economic advantage in working with the Russian defense sector. Susan Walsh, manager, commercial and international programs, and Tom Hajek, director of international marketing for Central Europe and CIS, United Technologies/Pratt & Whitney, stated that "under the old Soviet system, the military got the 'best of the best,' so in many ways it is easier to work with defense plants there than with commercial enterprises."

There are distinct assets within the Russian defense sector that make them attractive to a U.S. company, according to Frank DiBello, a partner with KPGM Peat Marwick. These assets include their brainpower, labor, facilities and plants, particular technologies, and specific products, such as planes, tanks, guns, ships, and missiles.

One of the major resources of these defense-related enterprises is their highly educated scientists and engineers. Jeff Baehr, director of advanced development, Sun Microsystems, stated that his company is working with a group of Russian experts who are world-class engineers. "Because they have had no equipment for so long, they are the world's best theoreticians. It is a privilege to work with these individuals who are so brilliant. They have just never been able to implement their theories in practice," says Baehr.

John Cohn, regional director for Europe, Rockwell International, verified this viewpoint, stressing that Russian defense enterprises have good technologies and good people, including capabilities in materials science, computer science, computational flow dynamics, and electronics. DiBello added that Russians possess sophisticated capabilities and technologies in a number of fields, such as biomedical research, artificial intelligence, and advanced sensors. As an illustration, 15,000 patents have been sought annually in the FSU biomedical field, but only 2,000 of these have been granted, because the FSU could not afford to develop all these technologies. American companies may now gain access to these technologies, which could lead to the development of new competitive products in a number of fields, according to several U.S. industry experts.

The above views were reinforced by many U.S. corporate representatives, who said they were attracted to working with Russian specialists, not only by their high level of qualifications, but also by the lower costs of research and development there. Dr. Richard Garwin, IBM, said that anybody in research and development at IBM who can get work done better and quicker in Russia is encouraged to do so. Although IBM has not set aside specific company funds, they are using Russian nuclear scientists, as well as other specialists from the Russian Academy of Sciences, to carry out research and development projects.

Other U.S. business leaders stated that Russia has a comparative advantage arising from its lower overall labor costs. Moscow-based Angstrem is able for this reason to produce its components in Russia 30 percent cheaper than in Asia. Polaroid has found it economically advantageous to establish a camera assembly line within a Moscow aerospace plant because of its lower labor costs and skilled work force. Although Polaroid has had to provide additional training for these employees, it has found them to be highly motivated and willing to learn. The cameras assembled in Moscow meet world- class standards, according to George Marquardt, managing director for Polaroid in Moscow.

Defense enterprises in the FSU are also better equipped than civilian enterprises. Many U.S. corporate representatives also pointed out that a lot of the equipment in defense plants appears to be outdated, often 20 to 30 years behind American plants. Still, there are exceptions. Robert Lewicki of C.J. Edwards said that he has found technology and equipment in defense plants that could not be easily or economically duplicated in the United States, such as a 75,000-ton forger that would cost at least $30 million to build today. Defense-related enterprises also have access to important strategic resources, including aluminum, magnesium, and titanium, among others. These are the types of resources and capabilities that a Russian defense enterprise is able to bring to a joint business venture, according to Lewicki.

U.S. international business experts also point out that FSU defense plants are advantageously situated in relation to the local infrastructure, which is critically important to doing business there. They have access to better telecommunications, water and sewer facilities, electricity, seaports, roads, railroads, and airports. All these factors are important components in an American firm's decision to invest in Russia.

Second, there may be a direct economic incentive to doing business with Russian defense enterprises, especially if such projects involve conversion. However, U.S. business leaders and corporate representatives stressed that no American company chooses to do "conversion" for conversion's sake in Russia. Tom Hajek explained that no company will become involved in a project if it requires conversion of defense facilities unless it makes business sense. U.S. firms that end up doing projects that are considered "defense conversion" do so because that is what is required in order for the project to be commercially feasible.

At the same time, U.S. executives said that if an economic incentive is provided by any of the various agencies concerned (U.S., Russian, and/or international), they would be more interested in considering conversion projects. Thus, one of the reasons for current U.S. business interest in Russian defense conversion is the availability of funds to carry it out. This incentive can make the commercial difference in an otherwise marginal project, if it sufficiently reduces the project's capital costs.

Third, American business leaders recognize the need to assist in Russian defense conversion. They indicated that, as corporate citizens, they are willing to help achieve the U.S. government's aim to support defense conversion in these countries, but not if it requires an economic sacrifice. U.S. firms are ready to work with the U.S. government to identify attractive business opportunities in Russia that could also assist in defense conversion.

Nina Dimas, international program manager, KPGM Peat Marwick, said that the most persistent request she receives from Moscow enterprises is for help with defense conversion. Most of the U.S. corporate representatives who were interviewed would agree with these enterprises' complaint that they do not know how to carry out defense conversion. American business leaders believe that they can provide the missing expertise in the following areas: identification, screening, and commercialization of technologies; reorganization of industrial structures and redesign of facilities, production lines, and products; retooling of plants and retraining of workers; training managers in market skills and new techniques; identification of markets and development of competitive international strategies.

For the reasons given, many U.S. firms believe there are positive long-term business opportunities with defense-related firms, particularly in Russia, although it is not always clear that these opportunities will involve defense conversion.

Lessons from U.S. Business Experiences

American companies and organizations are working in different ways with different types of entities within the Russian military-industrial complex. The entities include ministries, enterprises, individual plants, design bureaus, research and development institutes, training centers, and nongovernmental organizations. Some U.S. companies are engaged with these entities through contracts, some in joint ventures, and some in newly created joint stock companies. Several important lessons have emerged from these varying experiences.

The first lesson is that in order for a U.S. company to carry out a defense conversion project, as previously stated, it must make sense commercially. Whether a particular business model or project could be classified as "conversion" often depends on the definition of defense conversion. Several different models, based on different definitions of defense conversion, are being implemented in Russia by U. S. firms.

One business model that is being used by a number of U.S. companies is to identify Russian technologies that can be commercialized. This model is built upon a definition of defense conversion used by many U.S. companies, i.e., taking defense technologies and moving them into commercial markets. While this definition is quite narrow in scope, many U.S. firms see such opportunities as the best way to make a profit in the short term and to help their Russian partners earn hard currency quickly.

Batterymarch Financial Management in Boston has been working closely with a select group of Russian defense enterprises undergoing conversion. These particular enterprises, which have been carefully screened by Batterymarch, are creating joint stock companies as a means of privatizing and attracting foreign direct investment. According to Vladimir Sidorovich, former Batterymarch director in Moscow, large defense enterprises should be divided into segments, with separate accounting systems and bank accounts. He argues that the profitable divisions of the enterprise should receive additional resources, and that the unprofitable divisions should be allowed to go out of business.

Typically, the joint stock company would be formed around a division of the enterprise that has a commercially viable technology. Sidorovich proposed that "a parent enterprise would contribute assets of the relevant division, and foreign investors would contribute hard currency and provide access to world markets. To motivate the workers, part of the shares of the newly created JSC should be granted to employees."

In evaluating the conversion capabilities of more than 100 Russian defense enterprises, Batterymarch has identified six prospects that meet its criteria for creating joint stock companies attractive to foreign investors. Batterymarch is also attempting to create a "Soviet Companies Fund" (of $100 million to $250 million) to attract capital for these selected defense enterprises. Although OPIC has agreed to provide $100 million in risk insurance to Batterymarch for its proposed projects in Russia, the company still needs to receive the proper guarantees from the Russian government, in addition to attracting sufficient investment funds from potential investors.

Reorienting Production

A second model involves the actual reorientation of the production of defense plants from defense products to civilian products. Generally, this model is based on the partial reorientation of a plant's production and the use of selected workers, although it could involve the total reorientation of a plant's capabilities. For example, one U.S. automaker is examining the possibility of assembling automobiles in defense plants that previously produced tanks and other defense-related equipment.

According to several U.S. industry leaders, this second model has been implemented successfully by a number of European firms. One German company is producing aluminum wheels for the world market at two defense plants in Russia. These plants formerly built aircraft and tanks, but they possess a disciplined work force and metallurgical technology which made them attractive to the German firm. Also important to its decision was the fact that the Germans found a Western buyer for the wheels prior to commencing production in Russia. This enabled the German firm to avoid the constraint of the nonconvertibility of the Russian ruble, because it was not initially selling the wheels on the Russian market. U.S. business representatives agreed that if Russian conversion products can be sold internationally, American firms will be more willing to invest in a defense enterprise because there will be an immediate source of hard currency profits.

The Polaroid joint venture "Svetozor" was initially developed to assemble cameras to be sold on the international market. While a small percentage of these assembled cameras is being sold within Russia, this has been a less active part of Polaroid's operations.

One important lesson from both the Polaroid and the German experience is that a particular product can be manufactured and sold while using a limited number of employees and specific workspace within an aerospace plant. Polaroid is using only 30 employees out of thousands employed at the enterprise, enabling it to handpick the best and brightest for its operations. The German firm did the same thing — it is using 100 employees out of 10,000 at the plant with which it is associated.

Employing a limited number of selected employees within a plant does not fit the broader definition of defense conversion that is used by experts such as William Perry of Stanford University. Perry defines conversion as finding gainful employment for people, but not necessarily using the existing plants or managers.

We have found no U.S. firms that have adopted this broader definition of defense conversion in their business ventures. Instead, U.S. business leaders claimed that the massive size of most defense plants, which often employ thousands of people, puts a premium on more narrowly focused operations. This point was made by George Suter, vice president for operations at Pfizer International, who stated that one of the problems in converting Russian chemical warfare facilities to the manufacture of pharmaceuticals is their large size and the fact that they are also capital-intensive. He explained that U.S. pharmaceutical plants are not as capital- or labor-intensive, owing to the high level of automation within the industry.

Beyond that, American business executives explained that the size and scope of most Russian defense enterprises make it extremely difficult to assemble an investment large enough to have any major impact on the financial and commercial viability of these enterprises. U.S. corporate leaders stated that the millions of employees in defense-related enterprises will all need to be retrained over a long period of time. The retraining alone will require a massive investment of time and money that no U.S. (or other foreign firm) is equipped to make.

U.S. corporate representatives do recognize the need to help create employment within Russia, although on a less massive scale. A number of U.S. companies are working on creative ways to employ Russian scientists and engineers. Since this is one of the purposes of the new International Science and Technology Center in Moscow, American firms, particularly in the aerospace industry, are seeking to work with this center (and the one being established in Kiev) and to identify and hire leading experts.

American firms are also exploring other ways to employ scientists and engineers from the FSU military-industrial complex. Boeing, the largest aircraft company in the world, signed an agreement in August 1992 with the Russian Ministry of Industry's Aviation Department to set up a development center in Moscow. The new center will initially employ 30 Russian engineers and scientists to pursue projects in areas such as airframe technology and wind-tunnel testing.

U.S. industry representatives said they have no trouble identifying the key scientists and engineers with whom they want to work, because these individuals have been publishing in respected journals for years. Individuals who are not so well known will need to be identified by other means.

As for broader employment possibilities, Glenn Buckles, senior associate, Booz, Allen & Hamilton, said that it is important to separate the problem of generating hard currency from the issue of jobs and factories. "Selling arms will not fill factories," he says. Instead, other ways of generating hard currency and additional domestic employment alternatives will have to be found.

One such alternative was suggested by Richard Lamb, president, Richard A. Lamb & Russian Associates, who argues that the Russians need to determine what they know how to do and then market it. American companies can help, according to Lamb, by selling or leasing their technologies to Russian enterprises and assisting those enterprises to manufacture and sell products domestically. Some of these products can then be sold internationally. For Lamb, developing local manufacturing capabilities is extremely important because this would create jobs, particularly within former defense enterprises.

Another point emphasized by experts like Maria Aronson, executive director of international trade for General Motors, is that if a large U.S. corporation makes a major investment in a manufacturing or assembly facility in Russia, this could attract U.S. components manufacturers to that region. Jobs would be created in the major manufacturing plant and in the component parts industry. In this way, the initial U.S. manufacturing investment would lead to other investments, bringing about a multiplier effect throughout the entire area.

Finding the Right Partner

The second lesson is that there is no single factor that will determine whether U.S. defense companies will make good partners for Russian defense plants. There appears to be no consensus on this question. Rather the answer seems to depend on the particular business venture.

William Perry stated that a U.S. defense company understands and relates better to the people and organization in a Russian defense enterprise than a U.S. nondefense company. He believes that a U.S. defense company can help convert a Russian defense enterprise if it is converting to a product that is appropriate to the U.S. company. If the Russian conversion is to a consumer-oriented product, however, U.S. defense companies may not make good partners because they do not understand the consumer market well, and their accounting procedures and other business practices will be inappropriate. Overall, Perry stressed that in market sectors where U.S. defense companies face difficulties converting their own production, they will not make good partners for Russian defense enterprises and plants.

Jeff Moore, director of European programs for Grumman Corporation, argued that U.S. defense companies would make the best partners for Russian defense enterprises due to their own experiences in trying to convert. Such defense firms could provide valuable expertise on what types of conversion strategies have or have not been successful.

What is important, according to Vitalji Garber, is that the differences between U.S. and FSU defense industries should be identified at the outset of a joint project. Then the advice and recommendations developed by the American side can be adapted to meet Russian defense conversion needs. For example, Garber said that U.S. defense companies tend to overspecify while the FSU defense industry does not. Robert L. Bovey of CONCORD added that "the Russians were years ahead of us in thinking about defense conversion, but did not have the resources to do it." Therefore, Bovey said that Americans also can learn from their Russian defense partners.

The third lesson is that it is often preferable to "greenfield" (build a completely new facility located next to the old facility) in Russia than to work within existing plant facilities. U.S. CEOs who have visited a number of Russian defense plants with product lines similar to their own, have concluded that some, if not most, of these Russian plants cannot survive. They are poorly laid out, possess a redundant work force, have a "topsy-turvy" manufacturing flow, and are unsafe. As a result, these CEOs argue that it is better to start over with a "green field" than to make the massive capital investment required to update the existing plant.

John Smith, vice president of Bain Link, made this point by stating: For an American company to become involved in a defense conversion project, it must first identify the asset that the partner brings to the joint venture. If a U.S. company invests in a tank plant, there is no tank market domestically or internationally. Plus these Russian plants may not be up to world-class standards. So there is little incentive for a U.S. company to purchase a defense plant, because it brings a lot of baggage. The asset (in Russian defense enterprises) is the people. American companies should therefore 'greenfield.'

In contrast to this view, Russians seem to prefer to renovate the existing facilities. This difference has been a stumbling block to some promising business deals, according to several U.S. business representatives.

Examples of Projects

American companies active in Russia are pursuing different types of business activities: direct selling or buying, leasing of technologies, manufacturing, and exporting. These projects are being carried out in a variety of industrial sectors, including aviation and aerospace, telecommunications, nuclear energy, chemical and biological materials, automotive, shipbuilding, machine tools, construction, and computer software.

In general, the greatest level of U.S. business activity with Russian defense enterprises is in aerospace and aviation. This is not surprising since one of Russia's major industrial strengths has been its aerospace industry. Russia is the second largest aircraft builder in the world, although it is not particularly advanced in avionics and equipment. A number of U.S. firms are competing in this market, according to U.S. aerospace experts, because the Russian aviation industry needs new engines and advanced avionics. As Joe Chenowetch, senior corporate vice president of Honeywell, said, "Just to modernize the fleet of airplanes that the Russians have would be a tremendous business opportunity."

One of the other major reasons that U.S. aerospace firms, including Boeing, McDonnell/Douglas, Honeywell, and Hughes Aircraft, are so active in Russia is because Airbus, their major foreign competitor, is actively pursuing business there. As one business representative put it, "We cannot neglect the FSU if our major competitors are there." In addition, there is a strong need for building new airports and renovating existing ones, as well as designing and implementing new air traffic control systems throughout the FSU.

American companies are pursuing a number of specific opportunities in the following sectors:

Aviation and Aerospace: Booz, Allen & Hamilton, in collaboration with Steptoe and Johnson and Ameritrade, is working with the Mil Helicopter Design Bureau on the marketing of its MI-26 heavy-lift helicopter. The same three firms are also working with Vympel Corp. (the Russian producer of their "star wars" technology). Vympel has the telecommunications capability to set up cellular phone systems, and it possesses a phased-array antenna that works off satellites and can be used in domestic transportation systems. Such antennae can be produced cheaply in Russia, so U.S. firms are examining the possibility of commercializing this technology for sale domestically and internationally.

One U.S. company wants to help put automatic test equipment in Soviet MIGs. A Russian plant that produces automatic testing equipment could be used to manufacture high-quality equipment with the assistance of this

American company. The U.S. company would help to produce and market the equipment in Russia, particularly for use in civilian aircraft.

Boeing has been sending some of its aerospace products to a Russian wind-tunnel facility for testing. This facility was previously used for defense testing.

Westinghouse Electric Corporation signed an agreement in late 1990 with the Aeronavigatsia State Research and Development Institute (ASRDI), while the Soviet Union was still intact, to conduct a "USSR National Air Traffic Management System Modernization Study" and to develop a 13-year implementation plan. Westinghouse formed an international consortium with AT&T, Hughes Aircraft, IBM, Daimler Benz of Germany, and C. Itoh of Japan to carry this out. The consortium is called GATSS (Global Air Transportation Systems and Services). Their plan calls for opening up new international air carrier routes, including Far Eastern routes. The project is currently undergoing some revisions.

Raytheon is examining the possibility of helping upgrade air traffic controls, using 1970s technology to overcome any export control problems.

Group Vector is trying to sell a Russian military helicopter in the United States to the U.S. Drug Enforcement Agency.

Aerocon, which has experience in converting aviation defense plants to peaceful uses, wants to buy heavy-lift aircraft (Ekranoplanes) from Russia for design use in the United States. Aerocon plans to design an ultra-large heavy-lift aircraft using Russian design and technology, perhaps eventually manufacturing some of the aircraft there. These new aircraft could be used both for defensive and commercial purposes.

Another U.S. company is examining ways to market the Russian Ekranoplane, particularly in countries such as Taiwan and Singapore that are surrounded by water. The plane may have commercial potential, although it is not yet clear.

U.S. aerospace and high-technology firms, with assistance from the U.S. Department of Defense Strategic Defense Initiative Organization, are looking at the possibilities of leasing test facilities or buying military space hardware from Russia that could be used in the U.S. strategic defense initiative or space program.

The Soyuz space capsule, for example, could be used as a possible rescue vehicle and FSU ballistic missiles might be used as commercial launch vehicles.

U.S. firms, such as Kiser Research, have been actively involved in helping the U.S. government and other defense companies purchase technologies for the U.S. strategic defense program and for commercial applications.

United Technologies, in collaboration with U.S. and Spanish partners, is evaluating a Russian ceramics technology developed out of the FSU space program, called "Self-propagating High Temperature Synthesis."

Loral Corporation, a U.S. satellite producer, and Fakel Enterprise, the Russian producer of unique plasma thrusters, have formed a joint venture to distribute and use rocket thrusters for satellite station keeping. These thrusters use weight-saving, electric propulsion engines in place of heavy, liquid fuel systems.

United Technologies Corporation's Pratt & Whitney Division intends to supply 80 engines for 20 Russian-made, four-engine Ilyushin aircraft. These engines would be used in commercial planes that have been bought by Russian International Airlines, a spinoff of Aeroflot.

National Patent Development has a joint venture with Moscow's Kurchatov Institute to market diamond-hard coverings for space, computer and other applications.

A number of U.S. companies are looking at the lower end of aviation production in Russia, such as metal bending, because labor rates in that country are so cheap.

Telecommunications: A U.S. telecommunications company is helping to convert two military satellites to commercial communications for use in business centers in Moscow. The Russian partner is providing access and right-of-way, technology, and security clearances.

Software: Sun Microsystems is hiring 50 researchers at Moscow's Institute of Precision Mechanics & Computer Technology to help design its new software and chips.

A U.S. company is working with a Russian defense enterprise to modify its software products for the commercial market in that country.

Nuclear Power and Safety: TRW is working with the U.S. government on joint U.S.-Russian projects in the area of "security cooperation," such as nuclear clean-up, which involves working with defense-related enterprises and research institutes.

Control Data Corporation is working on nuclear power safety in Russia with defense enterprises and institutes.

Allied Signal is examining the possibility of building a new facility in Russia to convert enriched uranium to fuel-grade uranium. It is not yet clear if they will use manpower from existing defense facilities.

Biological and Chemical Products: Raytheon is helping to destroy chemical weapons in the FSU. The Russians would like to find ways to recover one of the chemicals during this process and export it.

A U.S. pharmaceutical company is exploring Russian chemical and biological facilities to see if they can be profitably converted to the production of medicine, especially for children.

Automotive: A New Jersey company has an agreement with a Yekaterinburg defense plant to produce catalytic converters that could be sold to Western automakers.

Another U.S. company is exploring the possibility of working with a plant in Yekaterinburg that produces salt used in coating for cars. This could supply the domestic automotive industry in Russia.

Shipbuilding: A U.S. shipbuilding company has an agreement with a naval shipyard in Kaliningrad to build double-hull oil tankers. Both of these companies (U.S. and Russian) are undergoing conversion by reorienting part of their production from defense to civilian production.

Construction Equipment: Some U.S. road construction equipment companies are exploring the possibilities of manufacturing their machinery in Russian defense plants for use in local road construction.

Machine Tools: One U.S. machine tool company is considering a program to manufacture and sell machine tools in Russia in exchange for scrap metal. The metal would be sold in part for hard currency, and the ruble portion of the profits would be used to buy software equipment for a Russian machine tool plant.

Consumer-related Products: Infinity Systems, Inc. has been approached by two Russian aerospace plants to form a joint venture to produce Infinity's stereo speakers in Russia. Infinity is interested, because these plants are offshoots of the Russian space program and their labor rates are low.

Agribusiness: Honeywell is working with chemical fertilizer plants operating within the defense sector in Russia, helping them to export their products.

A substantial number of these actual or proposed business activities do not fit into traditionally accepted definitions of defense conversion. During the interviews, when U.S. business representatives were asked whether they were involved in Russian defense conversion projects, their first response was often "no." However, when they described the types of business activities they were actually carrying out, it became clear that many of these activities were directly or indirectly assisting defense conversion.

U.S. company might only be buying or leasing or selling technologies to the Russians, but these technologies were often being used by defense enterprises and plants to carry out some type of conversion. The full contribution of U.S. business to Russian defense conversion can be determined only by looking below the surface.

Constraints Faced by U.S. Business

U.S. business leaders argue that they face three major categories of constraints in doing business with Russian defense-related enterprises and plants. These constraints are related to: 1) internal conditions in Russia; 2) U.S. foreign economic policy barriers; and 3) American business culture and attitudes. While these three constraints inhibit U.S. firms from doing business in Russia, they also appear to make it especially difficult for American companies to become engaged in defense conversion there.

Internal Conditions in Russia

American corporate representatives stated that the fluidity and lack of stability in the Russian government not only continues to make it difficult to do business, but that this also creates a formidable barrier to working on defense conversion. Since conversion is taking place in enterprises and plants that are still largely under the jurisdiction of the state, it will most likely not succeed without the active participation and support of relevant government authorities. The instability and confusion within the government therefore create additional burdens on enterprises attempting conversion.

Continuing Political Instabilities: These instabilities also create uncertainties and other obstacles for U.S. firms that are involved in business projects that require or lead to conversion. Company executives point to the recent turnovers in key personnel in the Russian government, as well as the ongoing debate between the Russian President and Supreme Soviet on the scope and pace of economic reforms and conversion efforts. Such internal problems do not create confidence in potential U.S. investors, according to many business people. As Marilyn Pitchford, a trustee of Batterymarch Financial Management, affirmed, "if the Russian government could establish a stable government with clear lines of authority, and especially vis-à-vis Moscow, U.S. companies would invest there."

Absence of Clear Policies and Coordinated Government Roles on Defense Conversion: The Russian government's policies and lines of authority on defense conversion are still evolving. There is at present a great deal of uncertainty about the number of defense enterprises that will undergo conversion and the types of government support that will be provided.

The lack of clear policy guidelines is also reflected in the absence of coordinated government roles on defense conversion. In Russia, there are different and often competing departments in charge of various aspects of defense conversion. Jack Tymann, president, Westinghouse Electric Co., said that one of the major problems in working on defense conversion is that "it is not always clear who is in charge." This was affirmed by Joseph Chenowetch of Honeywell who said that "it is difficult to see who can make a decision (on conversion)."

According to most U.S. corporate representatives who were interviewed, their companies need more information on Russian policies and decision-making processes regarding defense conversion. If conversion is indeed a top government priority, U.S. business expects timely information on the kinds of conversion projects that will receive attention and support from the relevant government authorities at all levels.

Absence of Stable Regulatory Framework: U.S. business leaders stated they are still reluctant to make substantial investments in Russia, particularly in conversion-related projects, without the establishment of sound economic reforms and the necessary legal and regulatory frameworks. These issues are closely related to the issue of political stability, with American corporate representatives expressing a number of concerns about the pace and scope of ongoing economic reforms.

The incoherence of the legal and regulatory infrastructure continues to be an obstacle for U.S. firms. Laws and regulations governing the ownership of property, as well as the ownership of technology, are basic to successful defense conversion. The question "who owns what" must be resolved before a substantial number of U.S. firms will invest in defense enterprises, according to Marilyn Pitchford of Batterymarch.

American high-technology companies in particular express concerns over the ownership of technology and patents in Russia. A number of U.S. corporate representatives from this industry gave examples of technologies that have been offered for sale by various Russian defense-related enterprises and institutes. While the particular enterprise or institute indicated that it had the right to sell the technology, this was not always clear; in some cases, it was later shown to be untrue. Doubts about ownership create a great deal of uncertainty for American companies interested in buying, leasing, or investing in Russian technology. According to several U.S. legal experts, this is also a major obstacle to ascertaining the value of assets that an enterprise may bring to a joint venture or other business arrangement.

Since a large percentage of Russian defense enterprises will eventually be privatized, this should resolve many of the questions about the ownership of facilities and technologies. For the present, however, there is an undeniable ownership barrier to many otherwise attractive transactions with U.S. firms.

Another obstacle for U.S. firms is uncertainty about currency regulations for foreigners. A law signed by President Yeltsin in October 1992 requires all Russian resident companies to sell 50 percent of their hard currency to the central bank at prevailing market rates. This requirement exists regardless of the percentage of foreign capital ownership in the company. Many U.S. business executives said that they have heard rumors that Russian companies will soon have to sell 100 percent of their hard currency to the central bank, but this has not been substantiated by any Russian ministry officials.

The political dispute between the head of the Supreme Soviet, Ruslan Khasbulatov, and President Yeltsin over who will control the administration of taxes makes it similarly difficult for U.S. firms to determine, with any certainty, their tax situation in Russia. Acting Prime Minister Gaidar indicated in a speech in Washington, D.C., on June 17, 1992, that case-by-case arrangements for foreign firms engaged in joint ventures could still be made to obtain tax exemptions and special tax holidays. But the ongoing disagreement between the Supreme Soviet and the President's office has made it difficult to ascertain the practical availability of these arrangements.

Inconvertibility of the Ruble: The inconvertibility of the ruble is listed as one of the biggest obstacles to doing business in Russia. The Russian government's announcement on August 25, 1992, indefinitely postponing its plans to make the ruble convertible on world currency markets, has raised concerns among some U.S. business people.

The currency issue impacts differently on U.S. firms, depending on their experience in the FSU market. A number of U.S. firms have found ways to overcome this constraint in Russia. They accept payments in rubles and then either sell them on the currency auctions or reinvest them. Some are also using them to pay for supplies and salaries there.

However, new-to-market companies require greater assurances that this constraint will eventually be overcome; and in the meantime, they need more information and assistance on how to deal with the inconvertibility issue. These companies assert that if they are unable to take their profits out in hard currency, they will need to take their profits out in trade. This requires an understanding of how to conduct barter trade — an intricate business for which newcomers have no training.

Lack of Capital: Closely related to the inconvertibility of the ruble is the lack of capital and other financial mechanisms in Russia to support joint business projects, particularly those involving conversion. Without adequate financial resources, Russian defense enterprises will be unable to carry out comprehensive conversion programs. The absence of financial guarantees also makes it difficult to attract sufficient foreign direct investment, which is necessary to carry out conversion, according to many U.S. Russian experts.

Lack of a Market-oriented Business Culture and Environment: U.S. corporate representatives claim that one of the problems in working with Russian defense enterprises is their lack of a market-oriented business culture. American business people say there are problems in working with "old-style" enterprise managers. John Cohn of Rockwell International stated that defense plant managers "often have traditional defense mentalities." This problem was summarized by Kenneth L. Adelman and Norman R. Augustine:

> (FSU) defense firms generally lack the skills needed for successful civilian work. Their managers face problems at both ends of the business spectrum — in obtaining supplies and finding markets — and in between at running responsive factories. Workers lack the geographical mobility to adapt to a changing labor market. Like their Western counterparts, defense producers in ex-communist states lack knowledge of consumer preferences, marketing distribution, pricing and commercial accounting. They understand little of market research or turnover cycles, of inventory strategy or promotion. And in the ex-communist nations they understand nothing of capitalization, leverage, depreciation or product warranties.

As a result of their analysis, Adelman and Augustine claimed that the managers of FSU defense enterprises are one of the major obstacles to defense conversion.

There are numerous cultural and communication barriers to be overcome in working with many of these managers. Several U.S. firms pointed out the difficulties in communicating across long distances and across cultures. IBM engineers and scientists have proposed installing an electronic mail facility for the Russian experts with whom they work so that information can flow more efficiently between the U.S. and Russian research teams. Dr. Garwin of IBM said that his Russian counterparts seem not to understand that this will require a relaxation of Russian security practices.

Other market-related concerns include the uncertain availability of needed supplies (an increasingly difficult problem since the breakup of the FSU); uneven production quality; and irregular timeliness of production. U.S. manufacturers state that the importance of producing "just-in-time" is not well understood in Russia.

Lack of Information on Specific Defense Conversion Opportunities: American corporate decision-makers said they need more concrete information on Russian defense plants in order to assess their capabilities to meet business criteria. Information is needed on specific plants, their capabilities and potential for conversion, their size and location, the number of employees they have, and their assets and products.

Another question raised in the interviews was the status of closed cities in Russia. It is not yet clear if and when many of these cities may be open to foreign business or how many of their defense enterprises will be eligible for conversion. One American CEO remarked that even after these cities are opened, it may prove too difficult to do business there if the location is too isolated. Since the sites for these defense centers were selected for strategic defense purposes, and not for commercial reasons, it is unclear whether there will be any viable commercial opportunities, particularly with respect to conversion.

In spite of the internal constraints identified above, there is an expectation among U.S. firms now exploring business opportunities in Russia that the problems will eventually be resolved. This expectation seems to rise and fall, however, with the latest round of pronouncements from Moscow. However, these problems were not cited by U.S. business leaders as the number one constraint to becoming more involved in Russian defense conversion.

U.S. Foreign Economic Policy Barriers

There was widespread agreement among the U.S. business leaders interviewed for this report that the major constraint to their involvement in Russian defense conversion is U.S. foreign economic policy. Six major problems were defined by American corporate representatives.

Lack of a Coherent U.S. Government Policy: There appears to be widespread confusion within the U.S. business community about the Administration's policy on defense conversion in Russia. Many of the CEOs and other business people said that "there has never been a clear signal from the Administration," so it is not known whether U.S. firms, particularly defense firms, should even be pursuing business opportunities there. This view was shared by a wide variety of U.S. business people, including John Cohn, who stressed that "clear policy signals are needed." Tom Hajek similarly noted that the Administration has "great rhetoric but no solid policy" on the issue.

Some U.S. company executives believe that the Administration lacks a policy because it has not defined what it means by defense conversion. According to Susan Walsh and others, one of the biggest problems is that there is no internal agreement within the Administration on defense conversion or on what kinds of U.S. companies should work with what kinds of Russian plants. Lacking agreement on the overall concept, it becomes difficult to develop or implement specific policies to assist U.S. companies to pursue conversion-related business opportunities.

Instead of clear policy signals, the Administration has seemed to be sending conflicting and often even negative signals. Susan Walsh and Tom Hajek said that "the Department of Commerce encourages, but the Department of Defense message is that 'if you want to do business there, forget about doing business here.'"

This reading of the Department of Defense was echoed by almost every U.S. defense company representative interviewed for this report. Many stated that they have been present in meetings in which Deputy Secretary of Defense Donald J. Atwood said that any industry in the FSU that is capable of producing defense equipment should be allowed to die. Gordon Feller of Integrated Strategies said that the "Office of Deputy Secretary of Defense has consistently given conflicting signals or has not acquiesced in U.S. company involvement with the Russian defense industry, particularly with respect to the purchase of its output." Jeff Baehr of Sun Microsystems agreed and said that the "U.S. government is operating on two levels: 'move forward' versus an unspoken policy to deny them (Russian defense enterprises) everything."

The reality behind these perceptions is that most U.S. defense companies are hesitant to become actively involved in Russia because they are fearful (almost to the point of paranoia) that they will alienate their major customer, the Department of Defense. Without clear policy guidance, U.S. defense companies in particular are reluctant to explore opportunities in the FSU. As Gordon Feller so aptly put it, "Ambiguity will always breed caution, but it will also breed lost opportunity."

Lack of a Coordinated U.S. Government Role: Another problem cited by many companies is the lack of coordination and duplication of efforts among competing Administration departments. There are many different federal agencies and organizations with some responsibility for U.S. business involvement in defense conversion in Russia — including the U.S. Departments of State, Commerce, Defense, Energy, Labor, Treasury, NASA, and Agency for International Development, among others.

Ernest Jackson, director of international programs at Raytheon, stated that many U.S. defense companies are presently short-staffed because of layoffs. Companies like his therefore "do not have time to run all over Washington, D.C., to deal with 15 little fiefdoms. The lack of internal coordination in the U.S. government makes it difficult and makes Raytheon reluctant to get into the game," according to Jackson.

Although the U.S. Department of State is supposed to coordinate U.S. assistance and support for defense conversion in the FSU, its work is not always apparent to the American business community. Joseph Campbell, first vice president, PaineWebber, concluded that "either the U.S. government does not want to do defense conversion (in the FSU) or it is not organized to do technical assistance (to support) defense conversion in Russia. No U.S. government agency is oriented toward doing defense conversion in Russia." As a result, there is a need for a "coordinated U.S. strategy for aid to the FSU including defense conversion," according to John Smith of Bain Link. Robert Morgan of Infinity Systems, Inc., added that "the U.S. government does not do things to make it easy to do business there."

Business people say that while senior officials in the Administration give lip service to the importance of U.S. business involvement in defense conversion in the FSU, in practice it is often difficult to receive concrete support or assistance when it is needed. Jack Tymann said that the only way to win large contracts involving defense conversion in Russia is through government-to-government cooperation. One of the difficulties that the GATSS consortium has faced in trying to move its project forward in the FSU is the length of time it has taken to get an intergovernmental group together to discuss the project. A number of the difficulties were on the U.S. government side, according to Tymann. Representatives of Hughes Aircraft also stated that they have had a great deal of difficulty obtaining high-level U.S. government support for some of their proposed projects in Russia, although their foreign competitors in Russia are receiving such assistance from their respective governments.

There are individuals within the Administration and Congress who actively support U.S. business involvement in Russia. But these individuals are often "fighting an uphill battle" within their own departments to develop and implement policies and programs to assist American business interests in the FSU. Bureaucratic constraints continue to exist, including the continuation of a "Cold War" mentality among some senior Administration officials as well as in the middle and lower levels of various U.S. bureaucracies, particularly with the Department of Defense. Business people assert that such mentalities and rigidities lead to bureaucratic inertia within the U.S. government, which is difficult to overcome.

Lack of Sufficient Financial Assistance and Guarantees: This constraint is considered one of the most significant problems facing U.S. business vis-à-vis its foreign competitors in the former Soviet market. Even though OPIC and the Export-Import Bank have been able to increase their capabilities to assist U.S. business in the FSU, American companies say this is still not enough. For example, David James, vice president of technology for Union Carbide Chemicals and Plastics Company, Inc., noted that one of the two most difficult issues "any company faces in establishing a business relationship in the FSU is obtaining financing, particularly investment guarantees."

Corporate leaders from a wide variety of U.S. firms stressed that the United States continues to lag behind other countries in providing financial guarantees, export credits and risk insurance for doing business in Russia. U.S. aerospace firms say that it is difficult to compete with the European AirBus and French aerospace manufacturers because of their ability to obtain financing, insurance and other assistance through the European Community and French government, among other sources. U.S. oil companies claimed that it is difficult to compete with other foreign oil companies for that same reason. Like arguments were also made by representatives from U.S. automobile and truck manufacturers, high-technology firms, pharmaceutical companies, energy and environmental firms, food processing manufacturers and the machine tools industry.

Lack of Assistance in Identifying Defense Conversion-Related Business Opportunities in Russia: U.S. business representatives again claimed that their foreign competitors receive more assistance from their governments in this area. David James of Union Carbide stated that the second most difficult problem that any U.S. company faces in the FSU is "identifying the organization with which to work. With the dissolution of many of the Soviet ministries, it is very difficult to establish a useful and reliable line of communication and negotiation."

Some information on defense conversion opportunities is presently being developed by the IESC volunteers in Russia; the U.S. Department of Commerce's BISNIS; and the U.S. Department of Commerce's Defense Conversion Subcommittee. Since each of these is a relatively new initiative, the scope, depth, accuracy, reliability and usefulness of the information they are generating is not yet known by U.S. business representatives. Their efforts are considered promising first steps, although many business people questioned whether the Administration is coordinating its information-gathering activities and whether it is working with its Russian counterparts to identify and gather the most relevant information possible.

Two other interesting points about this issue were raised during the interviews. One firm that was interested in pursuing conversion-related opportunities in Russian chemical and biological warfare facilities obtained a list of such facilities through U.S. government sources. In the course of discussion, however, the company representative became convinced that the list had been compiled by the U.S. intelligence community for political reasons — that the U.S. government wanted his company to work with identified Russian facilities for political reasons and not because these plants would make the best business partners.

There have been other occasions in which available information has been withheld by U.S. government officials without explanation, such as data on airports and air routes throughout the FSU. Even though these corporate leaders are aware that such information exists within the U.S. government — the Central Intelligence Agency (CIA) and other intelligence sources have been actively gathering it for years — and it could be useful in bidding on proposed airlines projects in Russia, corporate leaders have been denied access to it. The same is true of information pertaining to defense plants there. Much of the information contained in the Department of Commerce's *Russia Defense Business Directory* was originally compiled by these sources and has since been declassified.

U.S. High-Technology Exports Face Government Barriers

A number of U.S. companies, especially in high-technology industries, still face official obstacles in exporting to the FSU. Three problems were identified.

First, there are still significant export controls in some areas. Despite the fact that the COCOM control list was shortened in September 1991 and again in June 1992, a number of business leaders stated that export controls continue to be an obstacle to increased cooperation between U.S. and Russian defense enterprises. For example, Chuck Frost of Tektronix said that the export control issue makes it difficult to even consider working in Russia because his company's high-technology procedures are embargoed under the Export Administration Act. As a result, he said that "it is not apparent that there are a lot of opportunities (in Russia for companies such as his), but we are trying to be active according to the rules of the game."

Second, business representatives claim that the COCOM control list continues to contain inconsistencies. For example, the list restricts the export of computer chips but not the computers.

Third, U.S. companies say they face a number of bureaucratic problems in dealing with the export license process. Jeff Baehr of Sun Microsystems stated that it has taken up to four months for his company and others to receive a response on a duly filed license application. Pierre Jambon, manager of international affairs, TRW, concurred that "while senior levels of government say that the government should look at export controls in a new way, this is not reaching lower level bureaucrats."

Other problems have been encountered with the Defense Technology Security Administration (DTSA) and the Naval Research Labs. For example, one computer software company wanted to hire a top Russian computer expert to help them design a computer chip. Individuals at the security administration expressed concern that the U.S. firm would let the

Russian expert know if the chip functioned according to the (Russian) design, which DTSA said would be giving the Russian valuable information and "teaching him something." This firm was accused of supporting urban terrorism in Russia, because it wanted to upgrade its radio network capabilities, even though this technology has been available for years and is not state-of-the-art. Examples such as these lead export control specialists within U.S. companies to say that the Cold War mentality still appears to flourish within some of these federal agencies — the attitude, as some put it, that a screwdriver could be used to build an atomic bomb.

Other U.S. Government Constraints: Several additional constraints were mentioned by U.S. business representatives. First, U.S. defense firms are still dealing with outmoded Department of Defense security regulations. U.S. defense company representatives who meet with Russian business people in their offices must still go through complex procedures of notification and reporting to Department of Defense. According to Ernest Jackson of Raytheon, U.S. defense firms have to worry that they may jeopardize their Department of Defense security clearances if they meet with potential Russian partners. Others are concerned that they might lose their Department of Defense security clearances if they travel to Russia to explore business opportunities with defense enterprises there.

Second, according to many U.S. business leaders, it still takes too long to obtain visas for Russian business people to travel to the United States. It is possible for a U.S. business person to obtain a business visa for Russia in one to three days in Washington, D.C., depending on the fee that is paid. In contrast, it can still take from one to several weeks for Russians to obtain business visas to come to the United States.

Third, several U.S. firms have experienced problems with U.S. Customs in dealing with exports to and from Russia. One American firm had shipped a personal computer to its Russian partner in Moscow. When the computer broke down and was shipped back to the United States for repairs, the U.S. firm had problems clearing the computer through U.S. Customs both coming in and going back out. These days, remarkably, it is often easier to deal with Russian customs officials than with the U.S. side.

Overall, U.S. business leaders argued that American foreign economic policy constraints impinge upon their firms' abilities to pursue defense conversion-related business activities in Russia. U.S. CEOs state that the debate within the Administration on whether U.S. technologies and expertise should be used to help FSU defense enterprises is not based on a realistic understanding of the nature or status of defense production in Russia. U.S. companies believe they can play a helpful role in this process if American foreign economic policy constraints are eliminated.

U.S. Business Attitudes Restrain Business Opportunities

A final category of constraints relates to the character of U.S. business: its attitudes and culture, including its organizational structure, decision-making processes, and experience in the FSU. American companies recognize that some of the difficulties they face in doing business in Russia arise from their own internal habits and practices. Four major problems were identified during the interviews with U.S. business people.

Lack of Leadership: American company executives stated that there is a general lack of corporate leadership with respect to doing business in Russia, although there are individual exceptions to be found within the U.S. business community. They contended that the majority sentiment (among Fortune 500 companies) was to avoid taking the risks of entering the Russian market alone.

Inertial Management Practices and Attitudes: Chuck Frost of Tektronix said that U.S. management may be too slow to take advantage of changes occurring in the FSU. The structure and decision-making process in large U.S. companies often makes it more difficult to respond flexibly to what is happening in Russia. For example, a business representative from one large U.S. manufacturing company said that the managers responsible for making the initial decisions about whether to invest in Russia were "fresh out of MBA schools, so they do not know anything about doing business there. These individuals tend to be more risk-averse than managers who have more experience working in the FSU and who understood that market."

Several international trade specialists within large U.S. companies stated that their firms' internal divisions complicate the development of business prospects in the FSU. One company representative said that it is difficult to persuade the firm's operating units to pursue a business idea in Russia that they have not thought up themselves. This problem becomes aggravated if the project arises from outside the company. In all cases where a U.S. firm has successfully developed and implemented a project in Russia, there has been an internal champion within the company fighting for the project's approval. According to U.S. business specialists, the need for a champion is even more critical when the project involves defense conversion, since such a strategy may not appear to have direct or immediate profit-making relevance to the U.S. firm.

Corporate representatives who recognize the opportunities in Russia find that they often have difficulties convincing their firm's upper management to take advantage of them. One international business manager said that he has taken three trips to Russia since the beginning of January 1992, but is now running out of business development funds to pursue the project.

Even though the opportunity as he sees it is enormous and he is beginning to make real progress, he is having trouble convincing senior corporate managers to continue funding the project. This incident is not an isolated case, according to a number of U.S. business people.

Corporate representatives also complain that their companies often rely predominantly on internal legal counsel to advise them on how to carry out business transactions in Russia. One business person stated that this was naive on the part of U.S. firms — that it is more important to rely on area specialists to ensure that the business venture is structured properly and that "they are getting to the right people." Again, this appears to be a sign of corporate reticence, of "playing it safe" rather than seizing initiatives.

Risk-Averse Behavior: One senior business development officer was asked by his firm's lawyers and accountants "what are the chances of making money in Russia?" He replied that the chances are between zero and one hundred percent. The firm's management was not comfortable with this range because it did not assure the earning of profits in hard currency in the short term. Part of the problem here is that U.S. companies do not know what to do with the rubles they may earn in Russia. Many companies prefer to wait until the ruble inconvertibility problem is resolved.

Rick Lamb argues, "U.S. companies cannot wait and walk into Russia in five years and get the market. They need to take the risk now." He believes that one reason American companies are afraid to take this risk is their general insecurity in the global market. U.S. companies often prefer to do business in Russia through European subsidiaries or other companies. But Lamb said this "throws away a major strategic advantage that we are Americans." Russians in particular show a preference for doing business with Americans, although this attitude could change if a large number of U.S. firms continue to visit Russian plants "to kick the tires" and not to pursue serious business deals.

Lamb claimed that one reason why Tandem Computer was successful in selling an integrated computer with software to a Russian bank was because the sale was made through Tandem's U.S. headquarters and not from the European headquarters. Even though the sale took over two years to complete, Tandem was successful, according to Lamb, because it listened to the Russian customer and because its strategy was based on the long-term benefits of doing business there.

Lack of Patient Capital: Many U.S. firms are reluctant to take a long-term perspective on doing business in Russia. American business representatives admit that U.S. companies lack "patient capital" (in which profits are not received for a number of years) in comparison to the Japanese, Germans and other Europeans. U.S. firms typically believe they can make more money investing in a place like Spain, without adequately recognizing the far greater opportunities available over time in the comparatively huge and underdeveloped markets of Russia.

Preoccupation with Current U.S. Business Conditions: A number of U.S. companies, particularly from the defense industry, indicated that they are presently carrying out reviews of their business policies and strategies with respect to the FSU. Company representatives stated that plans are being impacted by downturns in the U.S. economy and defense spending. It is unclear at present how far they will choose to take part in Russian defense conversion when they themselves are facing the same predicament.

The common thread is a lack of high-level overall strategic planning on business development in Russia. Given the current economic uncertainty and the pattern of risk-averse behavior by U.S. firms, the stimulative or path-clearing role of the U.S. government becomes even more critical. As Ron Covais, corporate director of international business at General Dynamics, stated, "We do not want to get ahead or lag behind U.S. government policy, because our company does not do business in a vacuum."

Overall, U.S. business leaders and other qualified experts contend that the continuation of "business as usual" will not achieve U.S. policy objectives for Russian defense conversion. Instead, there is a strong need for a new set of policy guidelines and assistance to encourage and support U.S. business involvement.

U.S. business, and particularly its defense industry, has much it can bring to the defense conversion process in Russia — managerial experience, technical know-how, an understanding of markets and of venture capital. It can achieve what the U.S. government by itself can never do. But at the same time, U.S. industry needs the close cooperation of its government to remove the many obstacles that separate it from success in this emerging new market. Working together, U.S. government and business can help to encourage and support defense conversion in Russia. The time to begin is now.   ✦

14

Defense Conversion in Russia: A U.S. Business Perspective

Jeffrey Moore

D efense conversion has never been one of the more blessed phrases in the English language. To many Western business people it has, for years, conjured up images of large, unworkable schemes to force the defense industry to transform itself from the known to the unknown. From markets and products it understands to markets and products it cannot fathom.

Add to this often maligned phrase the words "in Russia," and you have an even more complicated picture in the eyes of Western business. Now it's not just a process we feel uncomfortable with, it's a place we don't clearly understand. At first glance, this is not a winning combination. In fact, all this begins to look like something that most prudent business people are trained to run away from. And that is what many have done.

Despite the best efforts of the U.S. and Russian governments to make U.S. industry comfortable with the notion of their involvement in defense conversion efforts in Russia, it would be foolish to predict that any government can completely erase the legitimate doubts and concerns that exist. With real questions about Russian legal codes, currency, tax structures, and export control issues (not to mention the ultimate success of Russian economic reform) still unresolved, it is best to assume that caution and concern will be standard operating procedure.

But even amidst the uncertainty, business is taking place. And much of that business is between American defense/high-technology companies and their Russian counterparts. So something, however small, is happening. And it is showing signs of promise. But is this "conversion?"

Unrealistic Expectations Have Slowed Conversion

"Defense conversion" is a loaded phrase. Both Americans and Russians have become overly preoccupied with the words and equally uncertain of what we can realistically expect from the process. To use an American colloquialism, "We are not seeing the forest for all the trees." For many years we have been lost in our tremendous expectations of defense conversion. Images of American and Russian weapons engineers leaving their past experience behind to begin building toaster ovens is, no doubt, alluring. But history has shown us something else. Conversion of the utopian kind has, most often, not worked. Yet often our discussions are still centered around such visions. These expectations have gotten in the way of our progress.

Part of our collective dilemma may be that we have yet to decide exactly what "conversion" is. A myriad of definitions exist, but it is not clear that either the Russian or American government has accepted a working definition of conversion that fits its broader economic, industrial, and security mandates. This is a problem. Since we have yet to define it, conversion becomes even more difficult to see when it is successfully occurring.

Add the fact that the U.S. defense industry is overwhelmed by the rapid downsizing it is now undergoing. It is, in many cases, a fight for survival, company by company. For these beleaguered executives to take on the worries of the defense industry in Russia often seems too much to ask. They have more than enough problems of their own.

This combination of blurred understandings of what we want from defense conversion and the historical hesitation to jump headfirst into the conversion enterprise would seem to make the American defense/high-technology industry an unlikely candidate for meaningful involvement in "conversion" projects in Russia.

Strangely enough, however, it may be that, even with all these draw-backs, the U.S. defense industry has an advantage over the nondefense industry in approaching conversion related work in Russia. As discussed, the American defense industry has never had terribly high expectations of conversion at home, and so it is unlikely to set excessive expectations abroad.

The legacy of attempted conversion in the United States is fraught with difficulties and failures. Much has been written on this subject, and the conclusions are all generally similar. The defense industry, overall, is not well suited for complete conversion, because it lacks the fundamentals for a successful transition. It is accustomed to working with only one customer

— the U.S. government. Therefore, it does not truly understand competition in the marketplace. It has a poor understanding of cost efficiency, because it has rarely had to worry about the expense of its products. The paramount concern has always been performance, not price. One can assume that the Russian defense industry shares many of these attributes.

While on one level all of this is quite unfortunate, on another level, there is a certain liberation that comes with the U.S. defense industry's lack of success in what we know as "classic conversion." Without excessive preoccupation with definitions and dated measures of what conversion ought to be, American and Russian defense/high-technology companies can find room to explore and create new paths of business activity that they find mutually advantageous and profitable. And if there is anything that high-technology firms in the U.S. understand, it is that there are many quality technologies and products to be found in Russia. They exist in laboratories, on factory floors and in the Russian marketplace.

The U.S. defense industry's longevity and competitiveness could be greatly enhanced through successful and meaningful collaboration with its counterparts in Russian industry. This is increasingly recognized and understood. To any and every extent possible, these collaborative efforts should be directed at increased civilian production in both countries. Joint efforts in the area of safe energy production, toxic and nuclear waste cleanup, and environmental protection should be of paramount importance to both nations' governments. But the allure of joining our defense products expertise for armaments production will also be a strong enticement to cooperation. Our governments would be wise to recognize this and to begin now to ensure that such defense products collaboration is a constructive force in our international relationship.

U.S. Defense Community Knows Its Soviet Counterparts

Furthermore, it should be noted that, for all we don't know about Russia and the emerging Russian business climate, the U.S. defense industry probably knows more than any other industrial community about its industrial counterparts in the former Soviet Union. Years of intelligence gathering and careful study of Soviet defense production have, at least, given us a fair understanding of who the major players are and what they are capable of producing. Taken in combination with the recent extraordinary level of access into these defense production facilities, American defense firms are in a relatively good position to make a determination of who their new Russian partners ought to be. Not all American business leaders now investigating Russia can make that claim.

So, it might be said that the defense/high-technology industry is becoming less and less concerned about the definition of "conversion" and more and more concerned with crafting business deals that work. And strong arguments can be made that this is precisely how it ought to be. After all, if conversion amounts to business and job creation which adds real value to the national economy (as I would argue it does), then the best thing that could happen would be the strengthening of an environment in which responsible business can flourish. Several steps which encourage such an environment can be imagined.

Comprehensive, Inexpensive Information Sharing Is Needed

There is no doubt that "who you know" is an essential ingredient in successful business dealings in Russia. But "what you know" is increasingly important. Keeping abreast of changing legislative initiatives affecting the business of defense conversion (Nunn-Lugar, Freedom Support Act, Russian privatization and conversion legislation, etc.) is a full-time task. And, since some of this legislation may include limited funds for the execution of specific types of conversion projects, most companies are extremely anxious to keep up to date on their status.

But there are other, and sometimes more important, information needs. Which Russian enterprises have been identified by the Russian government as high-priority candidates for conversion? Where are those companies located? What are their products and who makes up their management? Profile information of this type would be very useful. And the more information that can be accessed in one location, the more useful it will be.

What types of Russian plants, laboratories or research facilitates have already begun the conversion process? What are their particular stories (to the extent such information can be shared)? In short, what worked and what didn't?

Industry, especially the American armaments industry, could benefit tremendously from the ability to review success (and failure) stories. It is not unusual for industrial management to seek out a demonstrated road map that fits their own business plans for Russia. Sometimes those case-study success stories will exist and sometimes they will not. That's the risk of business. But if the road map is there, it certainly will be helpful for a company to know that someone has gone before them and persevered. And if the company has failed, it would be helpful to understand why.

Bits and pieces of this information can be found in many places. Conferences which bring together a range of experts and practitioners from both nations can often provide vital information. The U.S. Department of Commerce has also made great strides in its attempts to provide such information services. But it is difficult to name one place, one central information "clearing house," where the kind of information discussed can be readily and easily accessed.

And here another point should be made about the importance of "non-threatening" information. Many companies that are just beginning to contemplate a conversion project find it intimidating or simply too costly to gather information from continuously proliferating consultants, special working groups within law firms, and the like. Often they find themselves feeling "sucked" into a relationship that is expensive and that they do not fully understand. That is counterproductive.

Clearly there is a place for specialized consultants, law firms, and outside experts. And companies that are well along in their projects will continue to make good use of such resources. However, if the objective is to reach as wide a segment of American industry as possible, and to encourage large and small companies to become engaged in meaningful conversion projects both in Russia and the United States, an effort should be made to get current and useful information to them in as effective, coordinated, and inexpensive a way as possible.

Thought should be given to the creation of a "one-stop" conversion information clearinghouse, accessible to Americans and Russians. Government budgets in both Russia and the U.S. are tight, so it is unlikely that either government could single-handedly design and finance such a center. Better would be a collective effort on the part of government, industry and academia to establish such a resource. The American-Russian Charter of Partnership and Friendship could be used as the supportive foundation for this center.

A Code of Business Ethics Is Needed

The Russian-American business environment which we are witnessing today is a complicated one and it is increasingly clouded with questionable business practices. These trends are making some people very nervous.

A case in point involves a proposed visit of a Russian public official to the United States at the invitation of a private American consultant. What was most disturbing was the way it was advertised to U.S. industries. Industries were told that a payment of cash was required for the privilege of meeting this particular Russian. And it was a very sizable sum of money. The fee was to be collected by the consultant. The visit never happened.

Now all of this could be quite legal. But is it questionable? Yes. Even if such a practice adheres to the letter of the law, the overwhelming perception is that it flies in the face of the spirit of the law. And it is important to remember that industries such as the defense industry are exceedingly sensitive to issues of seeming impropriety. The last few years have seen some well publicized scandals involving the U.S. defense industry. And that industry, at great cost, has worked very hard to set its house in order.

So a note of caution is in order for American and Russian audiences. If questionable practices continue to run unchecked, large numbers of companies are likely to disengage from joint business discussions. And they will do so for reasons of self preservation.

The recently created U.S.-Russian Business Development Committee would do well to examine this and other issues of business culture and conduct. Both nations have much to learn about each other's "norms of business behavior." We would all gain with a fuller appreciation of those codes. There is much to lose if the current trend is not reversed.

Rethinking Risk: It's Part of Business

Successful business people understand that business is about manageable risk. Where there is absolutely no risk, there is likely to be no gain. But an often-heard perception about defense conversion in Russia is that there is a disproportionate amount of risk in comparison to near-term gain. In some cases this is true.

We all know there is risk to business in Russia; there is little that is new in this argument. Perceptions of risk, however, play a peculiar role with the American defense industry. There is risk that this industry understands and works with all the time — technology risk. Technology risk is what the defense industry prefers to call a technology challenge. More times than not, it faces up to those challenges and overcomes them. And, if it is being paid to meet a particular technology challenge (normally by the U.S. government), then there's "nothing it can't do."

But the story is significantly different when risk manifests itself both in questions concerning the potential customer ("We've never dealt with these people before."), or when the product, no matter how simple, is not well understood ("We know how to make airplanes, we don't know how to make baby carriages."). This typifies the historical American response to defense conversion.

But experience is showing that there is another approach to understanding and working with risk. And this approach bodes well for the success of conversion projects both in the United States and in Russia.

The trick is not to decouple technology challenges from the work of defense conversion. In fact, those challenges ought to be highlighted because this particular kind of challenge (or what others might call risk) is what defense industry management understands and feels compelled by. So don't ask airplane builders to stop building airplanes or engineers to start designing hubcaps from titanium. Instead, governments and industrial management should be encouraging defense companies to put their significant skills and technical knowhow to work in addressing the new challenges of a changing planet: environmental cleanup and monitoring systems; nuclear waste disposal; safer energy production; and more efficient modes of transportation.

These are logical outgrowths of technologies that, in many cases, we already understand and have worked with. With this familiarity comes a new level of comfort. That is key to taking the next step — venturing into a market (be it in Russia, the U.S., or anywhere else in the world) that we don't yet clearly understand.

Is there still risk? Yes. But with each day, the risk becomes more manageable. And where risk can be managed, there is likely to be success.

Joint Russian-U.S. Declaration on Defense Conversion

Signed by Presidents Bush and Yeltsin, June 17, 1992 Summit

The United States of America and the Russian Federation recognize that defense conversion is a key challenge of the post-Cold War era and essential for building democratic peace. Both parties realize the hardships involved in defense conversion efforts. But the parties realize, too, that the successful conversion of resources no longer needed for defense is in the long-term economic and national security interests of their peoples. Therefore, the United State of America and the Russian Federation declare their intention to devote priority to cooperation in advancing defense conversion.

Recognizing the important role of the private sector and of practical participation by business communities in the complex task of defense conversion, the United States of America and the Russian Federation are establishing a U.S. - Russian Defense Conversion Committee to facilitate conversion through expanded trade and investment. The intergovernmental committee will be established within the framework of the U.S. - Russia Business Development Committee and will be designed to facilitate the exchange of information and the promotion of trade and investment, including through the development of contacts between interested groups, the expansion of information exchange on enterprises undergoing conversion, and the improvement of conditions for commercial activities in both countries through the identification and removal of obstacles to expanded trade and investment. The Committee will inform the governments of both countries on a regular basis of the results of its activities, in order that they may take timely and effective measures to eliminate impediments to bilateral cooperation in the area of conversion.

With the aim of promoting successful cooperation in conversion, each of the parties intends to take a number of practical steps in the near future.

The Russian Federation intends to establish on its territory a favorable political, economic, legal, and regulatory climate for American trade and investment, including the adoption of macroeconomic reforms necessary to institute convertibility of the ruble; the pursuit of complementary microeconomic reforms to support privatization and demonopolization of industry; the enactment of laws to guarantee contract and property rights; and, the dissemination of internationally-accepted standards of basic business and financial information on enterprises undergoing conversion.

The United States of America intends to facilitate U.S. business engagement in commercially-viable conversion projects in Russia, including joint ventures, through the placement of long-term defense conversion resident advisers to serve as catalysts for U.S. business engagements and to provide expertise to local leaders and enterprise directors; the establishment in Russia of business centers with translation, education, and training facilities for U.S. businesses operating in Russia; the creation of a business information service ("BISNIS") in Washington to match businesses in Russia with potential investors in the United States; and, the involvement of the Trade and Development Program, the Overseas Private Investment Corporation, and the Export-Import Bank to provide incentives to American private investment in commercially viable defense conversion projects.

The United States of America and the Russian Federation endorse the COCOM Cooperation Forum on Export Control as a means to heal Cold War divisions and advance conversion through helping to remove barriers to high-technology trade, assisting in the establishment of COCOM-comparable export control regimes in Russia and the other new independent states, and establishing procedures to ensure the civil end-use of sensitive goods and technologies on matters of common concern. Both parties agree that this process is based on their mutual determination strictly to adhere to world standards of export controls in the area of the non-proliferation of weapons of mass destruction and related technologies, missiles and missile technology, destabilizing conventional armaments, and dual-use goods and technologies.

The parties strongly encourage the expansion of bilateral defense and military contacts and the work of the North Atlantic Cooperation Council in addressing the full range of military issues that are critically linked to the success of conversion including civilian control of the military in a democracy; defense planning, budgeting, and procurement in a market economy; base closings and conversions; and demobilization and retraining as well as social protection.

On Conversion of the Defense Industry in the Russian Federation

*Text of March 1992 Law**

Signed by Russian Federation President B. Yeltsin, Moscow,
House of Soviets of Russia, March 20, 1992, No. 2551-1.

The present Law defines the legal foundations for the activity of defense and associated enterprises, associations, and organizations in the conditions of the reduction or cessation of defense orders and the associated conversion of their production capacities, scientific and technical potential, and manpower resources.

The Law regulates relations between Russian Federation organs of state administration and organs of state administration of national-state and administrative-territorial formations, and enterprises, associations, and organizations during the conversion process, and guarantees protection of the interests of all participants in that process under conditions of market relations and the use of economic methods of management.

The Law specifies the procedure for resolving legal, economic, and social questions arising during the conversion process, and is aimed at ensuring the most effective utilization for civilian purposes of the production capacities, scientific and technical potential, and manpower resources of the enterprises undergoing conversion.

Section 1. General Provisions

Article 1. Main Terms and Definitions

1. In the present Law, conversion of the defense industry (hereinafter conversion) means the partial or complete reorientation from military to civilian needs, under the procedure specified in this Law, of the freed production capacities, scientific and technical potential, and manpower

---

* This is the Russian government translation.

resources of defense and associated enterprises, associations, and organizations.

2. An enterprise undergoing conversion is a production or science-and-production association or plant, design or research organization, or any other enterprise, irrespective of the form of ownership, that is engaged in scientific and (or) production activity for military needs (that is, the production, development, research, testing, maintenance, and servicing of arms and military equipment and of subassemblies, materials, and specialized technological equipment for them, as well as the extraction, processing, reutilization, and storage of specialized types of raw and semifinished materials for the production of arms and military equipment used by the armed forces, security organs, and law enforcement organs of the Russian Federation) at which the said activity is being reduced or terminated and where measures are consequently being implemented to produce civilian output and reutilize military-technical facilities.

Defense enterprises in respect of which a decision has been adopted to terminate their activity or to eliminate them due to the technical and economic inexpediency of redesignating them, are also defined as undergoing conversion under the present Law.

Article 2. Principles of Conversion

1. The reduction or cessation of production activity for military needs at the defense enterprise is founded on decisions by Russian Federation organs of state power, and also on the de facto reduction of military expenditures for these purposes.

2. The main principle of work by enterprises undergoing conversion is the use of the high-technology capacities of the defense complex to produce output capable of competing on the foreign market.

3. The production capacities, scientific and technical potential, and manpower resources of defense sectors of industry that are freed during the conversion process are enlisted to implement priority state-targeted programs for the socioeconomic development of the Russian Federation. Here account is taken of the requirements of the national economy, the proposals of the enterprises undergoing conversion, the scientific, technical, and production groundwork that has been built up at the enterprises undergoing conversion, the professional skills of the personnel, and the enterprises' specialization and technical equipment.

4. Enterprises undergoing conversion make provision on a contract basis, out of funds allocated for defense needs, for the creation, preservation, and development of mobilization capacities in accordance with the targets approved by the Russian Federation Government, and also for the

preservation of the necessary servicing personnel.

5. Conversion takes place in the context of full observance of all norms laid down by Russian Federation legislation for the social protection of the personnel of enterprises undergoing conversion.

Section 2. Organization, Planning, and Finance of Defense Industry Conversion

Article 3. Planning of the Defense Order and Conversion

1. Planning of the state defense order for the development, production, and delivery of arms and military equipment (hereinafter the defense order) is based on the military doctrine of the Russian Federation and its basic principles. On the basis of the military doctrine of the Russian Federation adopted by the Russian Federation Supreme Soviet, the Russian Federation Defense Ministry, with the participation of the relevant ministries and departments, enterprises, associations, and organizations, draws up long-term programs for the development of arms and military equipment and programs for the creation, preservation, and development of mobilization capacities. Similar programs are drawn up by security organs and law enforcement organs of the Russian Federation.

In accordance with these programs, long-term contracts are concluded and the defense order is approved. The said long-term programs are also used in the compilation of state conversion programs and are communicated to the interested enterprises undergoing conversion for the purposes of planning conversion and organizing production.

2. On the basis of the Russian Federation republic budget, the details of the corresponding long-term programs are worked out, existing contracts are extended, and competitions are held for the fulfillment of new orders.

Conversion is determined to begin in the year in which the production and development of arms and military equipment are actually reduced or ceased at the enterprises, or in which the redesignation of uncommissioned capacities begins.

Article 4. Conversion Programs

1. The main role in organizing the switch from military to civilian production and the drawing up of conversion programs belongs to the defense enterprise.

The basis for drawing up the conversion program at the enterprise consists of:

• Programs for the development and production of arms and military equipment and programs for supporting the activity of security organs and law enforcement organs of the Russian Federation;

• Programs for the creation, preservation, and development of mobilization capacities;

• The order for the development, production, and delivery of output and goods for important state needs (including defense needs).

2. The drawing up of state conversion programs and the organization of their execution are carried out by the Russian Federation Ministry of Industry.

3. Regional conversion programs are drawn up by the organs of executive power of national-state and administrative-territorial formations, and also by conversion coordination councils or other organs promoting the processes of implementation of conversion in a region.

4. The participation of enterprises undergoing conversion in state and regional programs is strictly voluntary and based on the principle of economic interest and competition.

Article 5. Finance and Material and Technical Provision
for the Conversion Process

1. The procedure for finance and material and technical provision for the defense order is defined by means of a contract between the executor to the order and the client, concluded in accordance with Russian Federation legislation.

2. The procedure for finance and material and technical provision for work under state conversion programs is established in the said programs.

3. The material interest of the leader of a state enterprise undergoing conversion in improving the economic indicators (including that of maintaining the level of employment) is ensured by the terms of the contract concluded in accordance with Russian Federation legislation.

4. With a view to ensuring credit availability and the implementation of state conversion programs, a state conversion fund is set up. The sources and procedure for financing the said fund are determined by the Russian Federation Supreme Soviet in the course of approving the Russian Federation republic budget.

5. Enterprises undergoing conversion are granted the right to form special centralized funds for the financing of research, experimental, design, and planning work, and also for the assimilation of new types of output. The said funds are formed on the basis of contributions for profits up to a level of 1.5 percent of the prime cost of the enterprises' commodity output (operations, services), such payments being deductible for the taxable base for the calculation of income tax (profit tax).

Article 6. Aspects of Reorganization and Privatization of Enterprises Undergoing Conversion

1. In the case of the full conversion of enterprises that belong to an association and are not legal persons in their own right, or of shops, sections, or other structural subdivisions of enterprises, they may be designated as autonomous state enterprises with the rights of a legal person. The decision to designate a subdivision as an autonomous state enterprise is made on a vote at a general meeting of the subdivision's labor collective, by a majority of the total number of members of the collective. Designation as an autonomous state enterprise takes place in accordance with Russian Federation legislation.

2. The labor collective of a state enterprise undergoing full conversion may submit an application for the privatization of its enterprise, participate, through its representatives, in the formulation of the privatization plan, and enjoy, in the privatization process, the privileges granted by Russian Federation legislation to members of enterprises' labor collectives.

3. In the case of partial conversion, an enterprise or its structural subdivision is privatized in accordance with Russian Federation legislation and the State Privatization Program.

4. Participation by foreign investors in the privatization of enterprises undergoing conversion takes place in accordance with the State Privatization Program, the RSFSR Law "On Foreign Investments in the RSFSR," and Russian Federation legislation on privatization.

5. Enterprises or structural subdivisions of enterprises whose purpose relates to mobilization and that are not used in current production are not subject to privatization.

Section 3. Social Protection, Compensations, and Concessions for Enterprises Undergoing Conversion

Article 7. Social Protection for Workers at Enterprises Undergoing Conversion

1. Citizens of the Russian Federation working at enterprises undergoing conversion and also those who are freed as a result of conversion are entitled to social protection in accordance with the present Law and other legislative acts of the Russian Federation.

2. For the workers at mining, metallurgical, radio-chemical, and specialized assembly facilities in the uranium industry who are freed as a result of conversion, the period for which an unemployment allowance is received may be extended by up to two years by decision of the local soviet of people's deputies.

3. Workers freed as a result of conversion who had worked in defense sectors of industry for at least 15 years are entitled to the use of sector social facilities and sector medical services and to retain their place in the waiting line for housing, and are also granted preferential rights to individual housing construction or membership of housing construction cooperatives in all regions of the Russian Federation.

4. Cities and settlements where more than 20 percent of the employed population is made redundant as a result of conversion may be granted the status of priority development territories under Article 17 of the RSFSR Law "On Employment of the Population in the RSFSR."

5. The dismissal of workers from an enterprise undergoing conversion as a result of conversion is, as an additional condition of dismissal, to be mandatorily recorded in the worker's labor record as a reason for dismissal.

6. The requirements set forth in Point 5 of the present Article also apply to workers dismissed in accordance with Article 29 Points 5 and 6 and Article 33 Point 1 of the RSFSR Labor Law Code.

7. All concessions stipulated for labor collective members by Russian Federation legislation and the State Privatization Program are extended to unemployed workers dismissed from an enterprise undergoing conversion under Points 5 and 6 of the present Article in the course of privatization of state enterprises.

Article 8. Compensations and Concessions for Enterprises Undergoing Conversion

1. Tax concessions for enterprises implementing conversion are established in accordance with Russian Federation taxation legislation.

2. State enterprises undergoing conversion are entitled, with the permission of the Russian Federation Government, to the accelerated amortization of a proportion of the fixed production capital, or—in the event of the complete removal of the defense order from them and the absence of the possibility of using the said capital in the civilian sphere—to write off highly specialized equipment without amortization.

3. Where there is a reduction in the order for the production of arms and military equipment produced on specialized production lines, in specialized shops, or at numerically designated production units, and also in other cases leading objectively to an increase in the per-unit cost of the said output, on renewing the contract, the client must, at the enterprise's request, revise prices for the output ordered on the basis of calculations submitted by the enterprise to ensure the production unit's profitability in the new conditions and to maintain the existing level of labor remuneration for workers at the said lines, shops, and production units.

4. In the event of failure to comply with the time scale stipulated in the present Law for communicating to defense industry enterprises the starting date relating to conversion, the losses sustained by these enterprises, including:

• Expenditure on the moth-balling and maintenance of mobilization capacities, social measures, and compensation for increased costs of output resulting from a reduction in the production of arms and military equipment;

• Sums paid in penalties imposed by suppliers of raw and semifinished materials and subassemblies;

• And other losses relating to loss of earnings for groundwork done on uncompleted output and the need to write off tools, gear, instruments, and equipment that cannot be used for the production of civilian output, are compensated for by the Russian Federation Government out of Russian Federation republic budget resources, unless other provision is made in long-term contracts between enterprise and client.

5. Provision is made for enterprises undergoing conversion that produce, under conversion programs, equipment and machinery for the needs of the agroindustrial complex to receive compensation for a proportion of overhead, so as to ensure that price levels are no higher than world prices.

Section 4. Enterprises' Foreign Economic Activity in Conditions of Conversion

Article 9. Forms of Foreign Economic Activity

1. Enterprises undergoing conversion are entitled to carry out foreign economic activity autonomously in accordance with Russian Federation legislation.

Enterprises are entitled to:

• Export raw and semifinished materials and equipment freed in the course of conversion—on condition that they cannot be used for the production of civilian output and taking into account the requirements of Article 10 of the present Law;

• Import new equipment and technologies, as well as subassemblies, for the production of civilian output;

• Transfer (exchange and sell), in accordance with the specified procedure, technologies, licenses, know-how, and scientific and technical information which, prior to the commencement of conversion, were used in the development of arms and military equipment;

• Participate in conferences, symposiums, exhibitions, and fairs involving the demonstration of new materials, equipment, instruments, and publicity materials describing technologies that were formerly used in the development of arms and military equipment;

• Develop, produce, and sell arms and military equipment under licenses according to the procedure stipulated by Russian Federation legislation;

• Participate in cooperation with foreign firms in the development, production, and sale of military output in accordance with Russian Federation legislative acts making provision for the protection of the Russian Federation's military-technical interests.

2. The activity of enterprises with foreign investments is regulated by the RSFSR Law "On Foreign Investments in the RSFSR" and other Russian Federation legislative acts.

Article 10. Protection of the Russian Federation's Military Economic and Scientific and Technical Potential

1. To prevent damage to the Russian Federation's military economic and scientific-technical potential in the course of foreign economic activity by enterprises undergoing conversion, and also to ensure the non-proliferation of weapons of mass destruction, the said enterprises should be guided strictly by restrictions imposed on the export (transfer, exchange) of output and technologies that have a civilian purpose but could be used in the creation of weapons of mass destruction. Restrictions on the export (transfer, exchange) of the said types of output and technologies are imposed by the Russian Federation Supreme Soviet and the Russian Federation Government.

2. In their foreign economic activity, enterprises undergoing conversion are guided by the following provisions:

• The export of strategic types of raw and semifinished materials and equipment takes place under licenses issued in each specific case in accordance with Russian Federation legislation;

• The transfer of technologies, licenses, know-how, and scientific and technical information for the organization of the production of civilian output and (or) their use in commercial and scientific and technical links with foreign firms are conditional on ensuring the protection of the Russian Federation's military-economic interests;

• The sale of other states of arms and military equipment and specialized systems, complexes, functional units, and assemblies that are components of arms and military equipment and also technologies for their production takes place in accordance with the procedure specified by the Russian Federation Government.

Supreme Soviet Resolution, Law on Conversion

Signed by Russian Federation Supreme Soviet Chairman R. I. Khasbulatov Moscow, House of Soviets of Russia, March 20, 1992, No. 2552-1.

Russian Federation Supreme Soviet Resolution on the Procedure for Bringing into Force the Russian Federation Law "On Conversion of the Defense Industry in the Russian Federation," No. 2552-1

The Russian Federation Supreme Soviet resolves:

1. That the Russian Federation Law "On Conversion of the Defense Industry in the Russian Federation" be brought into force from the moment of its publication, with the exception of Article 2 Point 3 and Article 8 Point 4.

2. Article 2 Point 3 of the Russian Federation Law "On Conversion of the Defense Industry in the Russian Federation" is to come into force from April 1, 1992, and Article 8 Point 4 of the said Law is to come into force from January 1, 1993.

3. In 1992, subsidies to enterprises undergoing conversion are to take place within the limits of resources allocated for these purposes for the Russian Federation republic budget. The procedure and criteria for distributing the said resources are determined by the Russian Federation Government.

4. The formation of a special-purpose fund to promote conversion under the Russian Federation Ministry of Industry in 1992 is to take place in accordance with the Russian Federation Government Resolution "On the Draft Budget System of the Russian Federation for the First Quarter of 1992."

5. The Russian Federation Government:

• By March 31, 1992, is to submit for examination by the Russian Federation Supreme Soviet the basic principles of the Russian Federation military doctrine and a list of avenues of activity in the military-industrial complex that are not subject to reduction;

• In the second quarter of 1992, is to submit for approval by the Russian Federation Supreme Soviet priority state conversion programs;

• Annually, is to present to the Russian Federation Supreme Soviet a report on progress in fulfilling state conversion programs;

• By July 1, 1992, is to draw up and coordinate with the governments of the CIS member states a procedure for decision-making on the joint production of arms and military equipment and on the conversion of the defense industry;

• Is to draw up and submit to the Russian Federation Supreme Soviet Committee for Defense and Security Questions in the second quarter of 1992 a draft Russian Federation Law "On State Secrets";

• Is to draw up and submit to the Russian Federation Supreme Soviet Committee on Industry and Power Engineering in the third quarter of 1992 a draft Russian Federation Law "On the Defense Program, the Defense Order, and the Status of Defense Enterprises";

• By July 1, 1992, is to ensure that amendments are made to contracts with leaders of enterprises undergoing conversion in accordance with Article 5 of the Russian Federation Law "On Conversion of the Defense Industry in the Russian Federation."

6. It is stipulated that the concessions granted to members of labor collectives on privatization in accordance with Russian Federation legislation and the State Privatization Program are extended to unemployed workers dismissed from enterprises as a result of conversion after January 1, 1990.

The Russian Federation Government is to make provision for a mechanism for revising records of reasons for dismissal in the labor records of workers dismissed from enterprises in the military-industrial complex after January 1, 1990, in accordance with Article 7 Point 5 of the Russian Federation Law "On Conversion of the Defense Industry in the Russian Federation."

About the Contributors

Vasilii P. Bakhar is deputy general director of the state enterprise Vympel, one of Russia's preeminent firms in telecommunications, radio technology, and consumer electronics. The major contractor of the Ministry of Defense's strategic defense initiative, the enterprise employs about 60,000 in Russia, Belarus, and Ukraine.

Sergei G. Chevardov is assistant to the first Deputy Minister of Defense, Andrei Kokoshin. A conversion specialist, he has a Ph.D. in Technological Sciences and is an expert advisor to the Russian Supreme Soviet on questions of defense and security.

Michael P. Claudon, president and co-founder of the Geonomics Institute, has written and edited numerous articles and books on international economic issues. He is the Dirks Professor of Economics and Political Science at Middlebury College.

Valerii V. Filippov is general director of the largest electronics enterprise in Russia, the Scientific Production Association or "Ferrite." Ferrite, based in St. Petersburg, specializes in microwave frequency instruments and exports to the West.

Sergei Y. Glaziev, a key economic advisor to President Yeltsin, is the former First Deputy Minister of Foreign Economic Relations. He was elevated to Minister of Foreign Economic Relations in December 1992.

Andrei O. Gorbachev, assistant to Russian Federation Deputy Prime Minister Georgii Khizha, analyzes enterprise solvency and provides investment assis-tance and advice to the military-industrial complex at both the local and federal levels. He focuses on transportation, communications, and space programs.

John B. Hardt, associate director and senior specialist in Soviet economics at the Congressional Research Service, has edited, coordinated, and contributed to many studies of the economies of the former Soviet Union, Eastern Europe, and China. He travels frequently to the former Soviet Union with Congressional delegations.

Aleksandr F. Kononenko, a member of the Russian Federation Coordinating Council for the Retraining of Officers, develops mathematical models and computer systems to support conversion, retraining, and privatization programs. He is Department Head of the Computing Center of the Russian Academy of Sciences.

Sergei V. Kortunov, Chief, Department of Conversion and Export Control, Ministry of Foreign Affairs, promotes the development of working relationships between Russian defense enterprises and American companies. He has helped organize U.S.-Russian summit meetings on conversion issues and helped establish Integration, a non-governmental organization specializing in defense conversion.

Sergei I. Kovalev, Deputy Chairman, The Russian Federation Coordinating Council for the Retraining of Officers, has been a privatization consultant for more than 20 Russian enterprises and through the Coordinating Council works to create new jobs for retrained officers in new small and mid-sized businesses.

Ivan S. Materov, Deputy Minister, Ministry of Economics and Finance, Russian Federation, is head of the Russian-American Defense Conversion Subcommittee, which promotes cooperative defense conversion programs. The Ministry attempts to create favorable conditions for Western private-sector investment in defense conversion.

Jeffrey Moore is director of European programs for the Grumman Corporation, the major U.S. aerospace company.

Aleksei K. Ponomarev, as director of the new Interdepartmental Analytical Center, develops databases, provides information, and analyzes defense conversion questions for governmental and non-governmental organizations. A principal goal is to encourage foreign investment in conversion of Russia's defense industry.

Evgenii A. Rogovskii, Chief, Department of Export Strategy, Ministry of Foreign Economic Relations, is responsible for promoting exports and developing markets for defense enterprises undergoing conversion. His responsibilities also include economic forecasting and the development of credit lines for defense enterprises.

Valerian M. Sobolev, engineer, rocket designer, and winner of the Stalin Prize for his scientific achievements, is first deputy administrator (acting governor) of the Volgograd Region. The region is actively soliciting Western investment and technical help to commercialize its defense-related high technologies.

Kathryn Wittneben, the senior economist for the U.S. House of Representatives Committee on Small Business from 1986 to 1990, is president of the Enterprise Development Information Center. The Center carries out research on public policy and business issues related to doing business in the former Soviet Union and Eastern Europe.

Boris D. Yurlov, Chief, Department of Conversion and Export Control, Ministry of Science, Education, and Technology, helped establish and is the deputy chairman of the Russian Fund for Technological Development, a non-governmental funding source for research and development. In the Ministry, Dr. Yurlov attempts to promote new technologies through new government programs.

About the Editors

Michael P. Claudon is president and co-founder of the Geonomics Institute and Dirks Professor of Economics and Political Science at Middlebury College. He has written numerous articles and books on international economic issues and is a frequent commentator on the reform of the command economies of Eastern Eruope and the former Soviet Union. As series editor, Dr. Claudon has been co-editor of five other books in the Geonomics Institute for International Economic Advancement Series. He has a Ph.D. from Johns Hopkins University.

Kathryn Wittneben is president and co-founder of the Enterprise Development Information Center, Inc. The Center carries out research on public policy and business issues related to doing business in the former Soviet Union and Central and Eastern Europe. From 1986 to 1990, Ms. Wittneben was the senior economist for the U.S. House of Representatives Committee on Small Business. She is a visiting lecturer at the Elliot School of International Affairs at George Washington University.

Seminar Participants

John H. Aguero, Associate, Burkhalter Associates, Inc.

Priscilla Rabb Ayres, Senior Advisor for Private Sector Initiatives, Office of the Deputy to the Coordinator for Aid to the New Independent States, U.S. Department of State

Vasilii P. Bakhar, Deputy General Director, Vympel, Moscow

George Bellerose, Periodicals Editor, Geonomics Institute

André Benoit, Executive Director, Canada-Russia Business Council, Canada-Ukraine Business Council

Edward A. Benson, President, Benson & Company Incorporated

Glenn A. Buckles, Director, European Defense & Electronics, Booz, Allen & Hamilton

Alexander Buyevitch, Russian Law Consultant, Chadbourne & Parke

Joseph F. Campbell, First Vice President, PaineWebber, Inc.

Margaret Chapman, Director of Trade Program American Committee on US-CIS Relations

Sergei G. Chevardov, Conversion Specialist, Ministry of Defense, Russian Federation

Michael P. Claudon, President, Geonomics Institute

Yuri Dreizin, Chairman of the Board, DYUAR Incorporated

Valerii V. Filippov, General Director, Scientific Production Association, St. Petersburg

William I. Fine, President, VISTA Incorporated

Barbara J. Flickinger, Vice President, Manager, Far West Region, Moody's Investors Service

Lee Frazier, Executive Secretary, U.S.-Russia Committee on Defense Conversion, U.S. Department of Commerce, Bureau of Export Administration

Thomas M. French, Chairman, San Francisco World Trade Associates, Inc.

Gene Gay, Senior Analyst, Science Applications International Corporation

Sergei Y. Glaziev, First Deputy Minister, Ministry of Economic Relations, Russian Federation

Andrei O. Gorbachev, Assistant to Deputy Prime Minister Khizha, Russian Federation

John P. Hardt, Associate Director and Senior Specialist in Soviet Economics, U.S. Congressional Research Service, The Library of Congress

William K. Harris, Policy Assistant, Russian, Eurasian, and East European Affairs, Office of the Undersecretary of Defense for Policy

Gregory Huger, Director, Office of Private Sector Initiatives for the Newly Independent States, U.S. Agency for International Development

Daniel C. Hurley, Jr., Director, Foreign Industry Analysis Division, U.S. Department of Commerce

Barry W. Ickes, Professor of Economics, The Pennsylvania State University

Benjamin S. Jaffray, Chairman, Sheffield Group, Ltd.

Robert A. Jones, Chairman Emeritus, MMS International, Inc., Chairman of the Board, Geonomics Institute

Yasuo Konishi, Manager, Trade and Investment Component, Agribusiness Trade and Investment Group, Development Alternatives, Inc.

Aleksandr F. Kononenko, Member, Russian Federation Coordinating Council

Sergei V. Kortunov, Chief, Department of Conversion and Export Control, Ministry of Foreign Affairs, Russian Federation

Sergei I. Kovalev, Deputy Chairman, Russian Federation Coordinating Council

Robert L. Krattli, President, Scott-European Corporation

Douglas E. Lavin, Acting Assistant Secretary, U.S. Department of Commerce

Lewis Madanick, Operations Manager, International Executive Service Corps

Peter B. Maggs, Corman Professor of Law, University of Illinois College of Law

Robert E. Marcille, Executive Consultant, Defense Conversion Project, Canada-Russia Business Council

Mark D. Mariska, Chairman of the Board, The Mariska Group, Inc.

Ivan S. Materov, Deputy Minister, Ministry of Economics and Finance, Russian Federation

Joan M. McEntee, Acting Undersecretary for Export Administration, U.S. Department of Commerce, Bureau of Export Administration

Jeffrey Moore, Director of European Programs, Grumman International

T. Scott Nadler, Managing Editor, *Post-Soviet Business Monitor* and *Post-Soviet Weapons Complex Monitor*

Rashmi Nehra, International Trade Specialist, Business Information Service for the Newly Independent States, U.S. Department of Commerce

Ronald B. G. Newfield, Engineering Consultant

Scott E. Pardee, Chairman, Yamaichi International (America), Inc.

Charles M. Perry, Vice President and Director of Studies, Institute for Foreign Policy Analysis, Inc.

Aleksei K. Ponomarev, Director, Interdepartmental Analytical Center, Russian Federation

Rodric L. Robinson, President, San Francisco World Trade Associates, Inc.

Evgenii A. Rogovskii, Chief, Department of Export Strategy, Ministry of Foreign Economic Relations, Russian Federation

Robert W. Schick, Senior Manager, KPMG Peat Marwick

Valerian M. Sobolev, First Deputy Head, Volgograd Regional Administration

Prescott W. Stone, Principal, The Halcyon Group

Vladimir A. Tchernov, Russian Representative, San Francisco World Trade Associates, Inc.

Richard Verga, Special Assistant, Technology Project, Strategic Defense Initiative Organization, U.S. Department of Defense

Natalia Volkova, Business Translator, VISTA Incorporated

William Hinshaw Wing, American Association for the Advancement of Science Fellow, Program Analysis and Coordination Office, New Independent States Task Force, U.S. Agency for International Development

Kathryn Wittneben, President, Enterprise Development Information Center, Inc.

Boris D. Yurlov, Chief, Department of Conversion and Export Control, Ministry of Science, Russian Federation